FULL-CIRCLE GOD

JED CHAPPELL

Full-Circle God
by Jed Chappell
Copyright © 2019 Jed Chappell

ISBN # 978-1-63360-103-1

For Worldwide Distribution Printed in the U.S.A.

Urban Press
P.O. Box 8881
Pittsburgh, PA 15221-0881 USA
412.646.2780
www.urbanpress.us

Foreword

Most of us have a date in our lifetime we can reference when our lives changed forever. Some dates we would rather forget, like the loss of a loved one or the date of a bad doctor's report. Others are dates in which we find joy or take solace, like the days our children were born or the day of a first kiss. Many times, the magnitude of what happens in a day seems too big for that day to capture it all. Take September 11, 2001, for example. Those 24 hours could never contain all that took place on that day or the resulting implications, for that day forever changed the land-scape of an entire nation and the world. That was and is the power in one day.

For Jed Chappell, January 20, 1995, is the day his life was turned upside down, only to have God turn it right side up again in the ensuing years. Matthew 16:25 reads, "For whoever wants to save their life will lose it, but whoever loses their life for me will find it." For Jed, pulling a gun on a police officer, being shot four times, dying and being resuscitated on an ambulance gurney, and then sentenced to 47 years in prison at the age of 18 seemed like the loss of his entire life. As Jed found out, however, God can take what would seem to be the loss of life and instead turn it into the very discovery of life. This book you are about to read truly is a "full-circle" story.

For nearly 10 years, Jed has been one of my closest friends. We have been friends, co-workers, and family vacation friends, and most recently I had the privilege of serving his family as their pastor. I have continually been inspired and in awe of how God's hand is on his life. For years, I have seen and heard Jed's heart, passion, and vision for the streets of Oklahoma City and beyond. I have sat with Jed at campfires, on beaches, in living rooms, on airplanes, and in cars, and listened to him share the dream in his heart. I've laughed with him, cried with him, and now I rejoice with him as we see his vision come to fruition. From drug dealer to outreach pastor to the founder of City Center in Oklahoma City, I have watched God restore to Jed the years lost to a futile and godless lifestyle. Through the founding of City Center, God is using Jed and his amazing wife, Julie, to bring relief and restoration to the same communities where Jed once brought destruction.

If you are holding this book or reading this foreword, do not let the contents of this story slip past you. Do not lay this book to the side and tell yourself, "Someday, when I have time, I will read this." You, or someone you know, need to read this book. No matter how badly our lives seem to get off track, we serve a God who can take what the enemy meant to harm us and turn it around for His good and His glory. This book will inspire, challenge, and leave you in awe of the wondrous works of our God.

Dr. Jon Chasteen
Lead Pastor, Victory Church—Oklahoma City
President, The King's University—Dallas, Texas

Introduction

I have wanted to write a book for the last decade, but I never knew where or how to start, and I was intimidated. How much should I share? Should I include names? What is the purpose of writing? Over the years, I have watched people respond to God's story that has played out in my life, so deep down inside, I knew a book would have the same impact as a live presentation. Even though at times I refer to it as my story, it is His story and we are to tell it whenever we can: "And they overcame him because of the blood of the Lamb and because of the *word of their testimony*" (Revelation 12:11, emphasis added).

I knew if there was any way I could record my journey with "pen and paper," then I had an obligation, even a mandate, from God to do so. Paul wrote of "the stewardship of God's grace which was given to me for you" (Ephesians 3:2). I have a story—many people have told me an amazing story—and I have a responsibility, Paul called it stewardship, to share it as far and wide as possible because it can help many people.

The story you are about to read offers hope to those who are hopeless or considered as such. I was a hopeless character and one who should not still be alive. I should be locked away in a cell and forgotten. Anyone and everyone who knew the old me had every reason to avoid or abandon me. The good news, however, is that God showed up in my life and proved He has the power to transform people.

Don't misunderstand—I'm not perfect by any stretch of the imagination. Every breath I take, the life I live, and the blessings I have received are because of Him and I am not worthy of any of it. The faithfulness of God in my life has produced clear evidence, however, that He exists and is ready, willing, and able to impact other's lives as well. God changed me so others would come to know Him. That is why I am writing.

On paper, I don't look very impressive. I grew up in a church-going home and my biological father was a church leader. I was the youngest of five children and when I came along, my father was overwhelmed and didn't know what to do with another little person running around the house. I don't remember ever having a conversation with my dad, who was a quiet man. Once my father passed away, I became a preacher's kid when my mom remarried. My stepfather has been a Church of Christ minister for close to

65 years. He led churches through the Civil Rights era of the '60s and '70s, breaking the rules of segregation within the walls of the church by allowing African-American people to come into the church—which was controversial. That's the kind of environment in which I grew up.

My life went off the tracks when I was twelve years old and stayed off until I was 18. After I was shot and incarcerated, I experienced many transformative mental shifts, experiencing what Paul wrote in Romans 12:1-2:

> Therefore I urge you, brethren, by the mercies of God, to present your bodies a living and holy sacrifice, acceptable to God, which is your spiritual service of worship. And do not be conformed to this world, but be transformed by the renewing of your mind, so that you may prove what the will of God is, that which is good and acceptable and perfect.

The business of the mind is to think, so as I changed my thinking, God was able to transform me from who I was to who I am becoming today. After my release from prison and during those transformative years, I was a pastor in a large church from 2007 to 2014. When I say large, I mean large, for we had about 8,000 in attendance at that time. I was the outreach pastor and we devised innovative ways to conduct regular and successful outreaches. Our strategy was to go into under-resourced communities that had zero to give back, so we were certain to show little to no return on our investment. We were giving ourselves away to people who were broken, hurting, addicted, and who had no resources. Those areas of the city were the same places I had poisoned with my lifestyle when I was younger.

At this large church, I led 600 volunteers every month as we reached out to our community. We established ten different mentorship programs for at-risk youth and under-resourced apartment communities. We led multiple outreach initiatives under that umbrella, including Sidewalk Sunday School programs, a Saturday Morning Kids mentoring program, large quarterly outreach initiatives designed to build community, as well as monthly outreaches to establish foundational relationships with residents.

From that position, I went to Minnesota for a year and a half where my wife and I joined some friends to help build a young church plant convening in a high school. That church is now thriving in a new building with more than 2,500 members. We're still friends with that church today, even though we left after a short period to return to Oklahoma City to start the ministry we now lead.

Now that I'm back in Oklahoma City, my wife and I lead a nonprofit organization called City Center, which once again focuses on under-resourced families. Our facility is also an at-risk youth center facility. We are in the process of switching from the label "at-risk" youth to "at-promise" youth because we believe at-risk is a negative descriptive. We want to instead emphasize that the youth have a promise for their lives. We want to bring them to a place where they can accept that God has a plan for them, no matter their current situation.

As I write, we have been leading this effort

for about a year and a half. We see 150 youth come through our Center daily and we serve about 1,000 meals a week. Rather than only meeting the immediate needs of our families coming to the center, we are working to see restoration and transformation occur. We are seeing people shift their mindset from poverty, lack, and despair so they can accept and walk out the possibility of success and hope.

Whether it is a mom who has been praying for her addicted son or a businessman who feels pressure because he can't accomplish some of the things he has hoped to accomplish—whatever the situation may be—our hope is that each person in the Center will see God involved in their circumstances and someone who is willing to help. No situation is hopeless, even for people who are incarcerated and think they have burned every bridge by the choices they made. I know because I was there, but God proved me wrong.

You may be alarmed or shocked by some of the violent situations described in this book. Be encouraged that there is a redemptive resolution to it all, and the stark contrast of what I did and what God did is necessary to grasp how gracious God is. The sin and brokenness in our lives are a vivid contrast to the glory, grace, and forgiveness found from and in Jesus.

As I write, I have been married for 15 years to a wonderful woman, and we have four boys in a blended family. The oldest is my son from a previous relationship. Our two middle boys are from my wife's previous marriage, and our youngest son is ours together. We met at church and her past is nothing like mine. You will meet them all later in this book, but right now, I simply wanted you to know who it is that will be relating an incredible story I have come to call Full-Circle God.

My prayer is that this book will offer hope to anyone who feels they are hopeless because they have messed up badly and are therefore beyond the point of receiving grace. The mile markers in my life are clear evidence that God forgives and gives grace abundantly. Also, I want every reader to catch a glimpse of the real Jesus and the truth of the Bible. Jesus is the ultimate Redeemer, taking what was once ugly and warped, and making it beautiful and smooth. Now it's time for me to prove to you that I serve a Full-Circle God, and you do, too

Jed Chappell
March 2019
Oklahoma City, OK

CHAPTER ONE

The Call

I had been a pastor for about four years in 2011 when I was sitting at my desk after one of our weekend quarterly outreach meetings around the Thanksgiving season. Whenever the winter months approached, I reminisced about that winter day in 1995 when my life shifted, first for the worse but eventually for the better. I had been out of prison for eight years at this point, but many of the events were vivid in my memory and will probably always be so. I was thinking about the officer who shot me four times as well as his family. *Did my crimes and this shooting impact him? Did they affect his family? Did he ever think about the shooting or me?*

Jerry was the name of the police officer who shot me. He was a detective when we first met, if you can call my running from the scene of a crime straight at him with a pistol in my hand as a "meeting." Jerry had been involved in a lot of undercover police work as a detective in the Oklahoma City Police Department. He was also a first responder to the Oklahoma City bombing. On that day in 2011 when I was reminiscing, I wondered what he was doing and where he was.

Jerry and I first "met" on January 20, 1995 when I was robbing homes in the greater metro area of Oklahoma City. I was carrying a gun with me and I was a young, angry man. On this day, my friends and I had a plan to enter a home, tie up anyone who happened to be there, and take everything they had. Thankfully, no one was ever home. During one of those robberies, Jerry shot me four times. I lost 65% of my blood supply and flat-lined in the ambulance for 20 seconds. That was when our lives first intersected.

I had no negative feelings towards this man at all; he was only doing his job. I was threatening his life and trying to kill him while I was hurting citizens in his community, but I was sure that this event had to be traumatic for him. I thought it must be difficult to shoot someone, even when that person is in the wrong. What's more, I was just a kid, only 18 years old. While I was thinking about my past and Jerry's role in it, I felt like the Holy Spirit said to me, "Jed, you need to reach out to that officer. Call him and ask him to forgive you."

My first reaction was to think, *Lord, I love the idea, but how is this conversation going to play out? Help me know how to lay this out. Do I just pick up the phone? Hi. Do you remember me? We had a little shootout and I was in prison for a while. I'm out now and I'm all better.* I might as well tell him, *Hey there! I'm a cannibal. Do you want to grab lunch? How is this going to play out, Lord?*

After that, I talked it over with some police officer friends. After a few months of deliberation and prayer, I decided to make the call, but I knew from the start it was God directing me to do this, and I should not have waited so long. My police officer friends also all agreed that I should call this man.

Jerry had retired from the force shortly after he shot me, so I had to find out where he worked. As I mentioned earlier, he was a first responder to the Murrah Building terrorist bombing, a tragic event for America as well as Oklahoma City. The first responders found harrowing scenes of small children and adults who were instantly killed by the vicious blast. I am sure that event, along with my incident, contributed to his need to get away from police work. How I found Jerry is another interesting story in and of itself.

A man who was with me on the robbery spree the day I was shot called me up out of the blue one day. I had tried to stay close to my companions in crime after I found the Lord to see if I could influence them to do the same. This man called to inform me he had found Jerry while he was working a temporary job for a heating and air conditioning company.

At first, my accomplice implied that I may want to carry out some sort of revenge against Jerry, an appalling thought I immediately dismissed for obvious reasons. (Fortunately, this accomplice has since asked the Lord into his life and realizes how wrong that would have been.) Yet, God used that man to tell me where Jerry was and after that, I was without excuse for not calling. I thought, *Okay God, let's do this. I'm just going to cold call him.*

I called Jerry but he wasn't at his place of business. A person took my number but not my name, which I thought was interesting. Five minutes later, I got a call back and it was Jerry. I was trembling and anxious, and my heart was beating out of my chest. I know my voice must have sounded shaky, but I heard the voice on the other end say, "This is Jerry. I received a call from this number?"

I said, "Yes sir. I don't want to take much of your time but I have a couple of questions for you. First, are you a retired police officer from the Oklahoma City police department?"

He said, "Yes, I am."

I knew I was showing all my cards with the next question, but crazy thoughts were racing through my head. *Would he hang up on me? Would cop cars suddenly appear in front of my home? Would he be angry?* Despite all that, I decided to take the risk: "Were you involved in a shooting that involved a youth in 1995?"

There was a sobering silence that seemed to last for much longer than it did as Jerry pondered his response. He finally said, "Yes" with what seemed like regret pulsing from that one simple word.

I continued, "Sir, I wanted to tell you that my name is Jed Chappell. I am the boy you shot back then. I was a boy then, but I'm a man now. I just wanted to really, I'm just . . ." I stumbled for the right words, even though I had rehearsed what I was going to say. "I'm calling to ask for forgiveness for putting you in the position that you had to decide to do what you did." There was silence, but I had momentum and I was determined to finish what was burning in my heart to say.

"It's gotta be hard to shoot anyone, let alone . . . ," but before I could get the words out, Jerry finished my sentence by saying, "shoot a kid?" And I said, "Yes sir." I didn't know how many years Jerry had served on the force and I am sure he had to build up a mental toughness to get through it all, but I could hear him begin to weep.

Words escaped us both as we wept and were unable to speak. Finally, I spoke up, "I want you to know that I'm a different man today," and decided to wait for him to talk, no matter how long the wait.

Before long, Jerry said, "I want to thank you so much for calling me. All this time, I felt like I needed to call you and ask you for your forgiveness for shooting you. That was one of the hardest things I've ever had to do. I have questioned myself. *Did I use excessive force? Should I not have shot him?"*

Once Jerry started talking, it was like the floodgates opened, which let me know Jerry had thought long and hard about the shooting incident. He went through a list of things he wished he would have done differently. After I listened for a while, I gently interrupted him to say, "Sir, you did exactly what you were trained to do. I was charging you while pointing a gun at you. I was threatening to shoot you. I was about to squeeze the trigger. If you didn't shoot me, I was going to pull the trigger and a stray bullet could have hit some little old lady in her bedroom or a child sleeping in his crib." It was my turn to prove to Jerry that I had thought about what I did for a long time as well.

"Jerry, if you want or need my forgiveness, you've got it. That's been a done deal for many years. If you need to hear it from me, then I'll say it: I had no intention of stopping there but was going to accomplish what I had called to do. "I would appreciate your forgiveness because I'm a different man today. I also want you to know that there are no thoughts of retaliation or bitterness. I am now on staff at a church" and I asked him if he had heard of the church, and he said he had attended services there.

I said, "Well, I'm a pastor there now."

Jerry said with excitement and perhaps relief, "Wow! God does work miracles, doesn't He?"

"Absolutely," I responded. "I don't know what that fork in the road looked like from your perspective after that day, but I would be honored if you would have coffee with me sometime. Then maybe we can talk about that fork in the road." At that suggestion, I sensed Jerry hesitate, probably thinking, *Let's take it slowly.*

Jerry responded, "Maybe we can do that at some point," and we hung up. After that, we would send each other an occasional text message to stay in touch.

About six months later, I invited Jerry to come hear me tell my story at a church where I had been invited to speak. He said he could not make it, but that night after I spoke, I received an email from Jerry at around 10 PM asking me to call him in the morning. Once again, crazy thoughts raced through my mind. *Did he watch me online? Did I say something wrong or something that misrepresented the circumstances? If I did, can I go back to jail?* My wife advised me to calm down, go to sleep, and call him in the morning.

I knew he was an early riser so I got up early to call him. I could sense a sad heaviness in Jerry's voice when he answered and he got right to the point. He and his wife had a close family member who needed help with a challenging addiction and he was reaching out to me to see if I could help this person (I don't want to share too many details, for that is their story and not mine to tell.) They asked if I would be willing to meet with this person and help lead them to a path of recovery.

I said, "Sir, there is nothing you could ask me that I wouldn't do for you. It would be a tremendous honor for me." I met with the family member for an extended time and I am excited to say that this person has been free from addiction for five years. It boggles my mind how one day I was lying on the ground in a pool of my blood about to die, but God preserved my life and brought things full circle to help me assist a loved one of the officer who shot me. That is why I have titled this book *Full-Circle God*. According to the world, guys like me should not have survived a crime like mine and go on to lead a normal, productive life. I have done so because God brought me full circle, and He will do the same for you or anyone you know who needs His touch.

Before we moved to Minnesota, I was asked to speak at a rally for police officers and first responders, before the recent tensions between the police and many of our communities. At this event, I shared my story and met several of the first responders who saved my life, along with the sergeant who booked me into the county jail that day, and they all clearly remembered me. The first time I was with those first responders, the television cameras recorded them putting me in an ambulance. Then at the rally, I took a picture with them like we were long, lost friends.

All this has been a surreal journey for me, and I want to share it with you. In the following pages, I will tell you what led me to run out of that house and charge the police. I will describe my time in prison and the days after prison that led up to my call to Jerry. I will share how a confused, angry, and lost young man became a pastor who now reaches out and back to those who are where I was. I know if God can bring me full circle, He can do the same for anyone. Let's go back to my earliest childhood so I can explain how I became the angry young man Officer Jerry encountered that fateful day when he shot me.

CHAPTER TWO

"God, Where Are You?"

I grew up in a family with three older brothers and an older sister, and all my brothers were volatile in many ways. My brothers were alcoholics and drug addicts who partied a lot. It seemed every family gathering ended up with a fight involving one of them. My older sister and I were close, but I saw signs of trouble in high school when she started running around with a crowd doing drugs. She was the most responsible of my siblings but was part of the drug culture as well. Lest you form a negative opinion of my siblings, know that they are followers of Christ today, living exemplary, holy lives. We have all had our journeys in life, and God has brought them full circle as He has me.

My family went to church on Sunday and Wednesday nights, and we were involved with other church activities. I wrote notes to my mom about the Bible, telling her how much I loved God and how I wanted to be a good Christian young man. I knew God was real and something inherent in my makeup drew me to Him, and I also knew there was a purpose for my existence. I am not sure how I knew it, but I did.

My older brothers saw the worst side of my dad who was a Golden Gloves boxer in the Air Force. He drank heavily before I came along, and I heard stories of him coming home drunk, waking the boys up, and lining them up to talk. He'd say, "If you're going to be men, you're going to fight. You're going to drink and you're not going to listen to anything a woman has to tell you." Those were his three characteristics of a true man. Unfortunately, that's what his dad and family had taught him.

Even though my dad was a tough man's man, he was quiet and a good provider. He drank, but always brought home a check so my mom never had to work. This was the type of blue-collar, hard-working man he was, raised as a sharecropper in Missouri. Even though my brothers were volatile, my sister and I always knew we were safe because Dad was there. Once we saw him drag my brothers out in the front lawn and light them up, but we were never concerned.

I was the baby of the family, and one day when I looked at my father as he was sitting on the porch, it looked like he was losing weight. I went to hug him but as I did, he winced and pulled away. When I asked him what that was about, he opened his shirt and showed me tumors all over his chest. It was then

I learned he had cancer, and shortly after, he died. His passing turned our world upside down.

I want to be respectful to my older brothers since they are all pastors today and have their perspective and stories to tell, but at that time in the life of our family, they were taking advantage of Mom. Life was difficult and she faced the enormous task of providing for our family after Dad was gone. We had always seen my mother's strong work ethic but then suddenly she had sole responsibility for all of us. I'm sure she was exhausted after carrying a load of the only provider especially after investing so much time and energy caring for my father in the last months of his life. Later on, my mom remarried a good man who was a pastor. After her wedding, we were off to Virginia.

One night in particular, a night before my mom remarried, stands out as one that shaped and formed me. The trauma stayed with me and shaped my perspective on life. One of my brothers was volatile, violent, and Dr. Jekyll and Mr. Hyde when he was drinking and doing drugs. He was, and still is, a skilled carpenter and worked on our family home. While working one day, he suddenly came charging into our living room. He took my mom into the bedroom and wouldn't let her out, demanding money for more materials.

Mom refused, saying things had gone too far and that she knew he was using the money to buy drugs, not lumber. He began yelling and cursing—his words were like daggers, piercing both Mom and me. I was hiding in the bathroom at the time, for we were the only ones in the house. I was terrified but I was also ashamed that I was so afraid. I was thinking, *What's going on God? Why is this happening? I grew up writing and sharing Scripture verses about how much I love You and how good You are. Right now, all I know is that we're not safe or secure. Why did You let my dad die and be taken from our family? Why are You letting my brother act this way?* Perhaps most importantly, *Why am I so ashamed about my inability to do anything about it?*

This moment shaped my thinking for years to come. From that bathroom, I could look out the back window and see the room my brother was supposed to be working on. He finally let Mom go and went to the back room where he was throwing things around while cursing and screaming. I was peering over the sill of the window when I caught his eye. He came up to the window and began yelling emotionally hurtful things that left scars. At that moment, I concluded, *God, I hate You right now. I can't believe You've left us behind. I can't believe You're anywhere near this situation.*

I was only 12 years old at the time so there was nothing I could do about it, but I still felt like I should have acted like the man of the house in some way. At that moment, deep and bitter unforgiveness took hold and wrapped their roots around my heart. Later, I was able to identify with the truth found in Hebrews 12:15: "See to it . . . that no root of bitterness springing up causes trouble, and by it many be defiled." That is exactly what happened as a result of my decision. From that time, I started hanging around with an older crowd in the neighborhood. We would skateboard and ride bikes together, and I began dabbling with drugs early on.

My mom is an absolute saint. She held on to her faith and prayed for our family as much as a mother could. She sought after God with all her heart after my dad passed away. As I mentioned earlier, she remarried a Church of Christ pastor, and I call him Dad today. After that, things changed and we ended up selling our home.

In Virginia, I began to be even more rebellious. I did not like my stepfather at first. The only thing I did not like about him was he that was not my dad and I was determined not to let him think he could replace him. We just didn't get along, so I decided I was moving back to Oklahoma City to live with my brother Joey. I was thirteen at the time, and I moved back to attend eighth grade. At the time, my brother was an active drug user and dealer.

I went to a tough middle school called Roosevelt on the south side of Oklahoma City. Even though I was only in middle school, I would steal my brother's weed. My friend gave me my first gun, a small 25-caliber automatic, advising me, "Jed, if you're going to Roosevelt, you need to be carrying some kind of protection." That friend died after being shot while engaged in some serious gang activity. He was a Southside Loco in Oklahoma City.

I know it sounds crazy, but in eighth grade, I was carrying an automatic weapon. I ended up getting kicked out of that school because I pulled the weapon on a kid who was threatening me for something. I can't even remember what it was all about. They never found the gun, but the officials knew what I was up to the whole time I was there.

Recently, my organization began partnering

with local schools to create Bridge Programs with their students. Through various partnerships we have with other organizations, the door opened at Roosevelt Middle School—the same school where I was expelled for drawing a weapon on a kid. The school was hoping to partner with us so we could provide some after-school services. We agreed to partner together. Later, I went back to share with the principal everything that had occurred when I was a student in 1992.

When I was allowed to speak with the students, I was honest about my personal story and my behavior while I was attending school there. I pulled a gun in Roosevelt and sold drugs there. Now I have the opportunity to speak life to the students there. I was overwhelmed with God's faithfulness to restore what had once been so broken.

I told the students at Roosevelt that they have a chance to make better choices than I did, and better choices lead to better opportunities in life. I wasted so much time when I was young, but I tell them that God doesn't waste anything, using it all to form and shape us, and He has restored the things I lost back then. Part of my restoration is working with people who are like I was, and God has used my poor choices to warn them not to do what I did.

I make sure that I don't glamorize my lifestyle of danger and drugs, for someone could think, *You had your fun and lived dangerously, and it all worked out okay for you. I have time to turn my life around, just like you did.* I share how extremely unhappy I was during that season of life. I was trying to do adult things by selling drugs to earn money and looking for affirmation I can only find in God. I was striving for approval as a young man and attempting to gain control over a life spinning out of control. I was bitter and I was in pain.

The alcohol and drugs were attempts to medicate the problem, a deep longing for love and affirmation from the true and living God found in a relationship with Jesus. This is the only thing that can satisfy our craving for meaning and love. I share my story with students to demonstrate that there are consequences as a result of our choices, even when God forgives us. I still have the wounds from where I was shot and those wounds have caused me problems years later. The physical challenges, however, are the easier ones to overcome. The emotional and mental wounds of regret are a daily battle requiring a decision that I must overcome.

Around the time I was expelled from Roosevelt, my mom and stepdad moved from Virginia to McLean, Texas, which is a little closer to Oklahoma City, so they could be closer to me. They were concerned and knew I was running on a downward path that was spiraling out of control. They let me move in with my brother thinking he would act more like a father figure because he was more closely related to my biological father. That didn't work.

After I was expelled, I moved to McLean, which was a town of about 3,600 people at the time. It was a bad move. I was a young city punk who thought he was as hard and tough as he could be, so I proceeded to break into every store in that town. I told a few kids the reason I was kicked out of school in Oklahoma City, so that put a black mark on my reputation. After that, I hung out with all the "misfits" in town. I began traveling to Oklahoma City to pick up pounds of weed to bring back to McLean, selling it for a substantial profit.

During one of my store break-ins, I got caught and was put on probation, being released two years later when I was 16. By this time, I was fighting with my stepdad all the time and hated living in McLean. I wanted to live in the city on my own and warned my mom that as soon as I was off probation, I was moving back to the city—and I did.

When I moved back, I was picking up pounds of marijuana and selling it for my brother. Shortly after that, I moved on to ounces and quarter pounds of methamphetamines. I was helping myself to the drugs, along with my brother, and I got wrapped up in the dope game. Once again, I started carrying a gun and always had a wad of cash in my pocket. I would sell anything I could get my hands on to get more weed and more methamphetamines, which were my primary drugs.

I was blowing through money and was the life of any party. It made me feel good for a moment when I spent all kinds of money on my friends, but it was all short-lived for I was lost, angry, and bitter. There is a rule that no one should get high on his own supply because he won't make any money that way. As fast as I would make money, however, I would spend it—and I was using my supply.

I would get a small amount of money every month from my father's life insurance policy. It wasn't much at all, but I would use that as some of my foundation money to buy dope and then sell it. I did that from ages 16 to 18. I lived in my apartment and continued to spiral downward. I plunged deeper into a lifestyle marked by anger and violence. I was collecting and carrying guns and selling drugs to a specific circle of people on the northwest side of Oklahoma City. All of that was leading up to that fateful January day when I ended up lying in a pool of my blood.

CHAPTER THREE

The Day

After January 20, 1995, my life would never be the same, even though I was only 18 years old. In the drug world, there are often drought seasons, times of the year when for various reasons—law enforcement crackdowns or other factors—the supply of drugs to a certain region is limited. For me, that was a big problem because as fast as I would make money, I spent it, so I needed a constant stream of income.

On January 20, I was in one of those drought seasons, and my friends and girlfriend knew this. Her two cousins and a brother pulled up to my house one day and said, "You have the gun. You need money. We need money. We have a car. Let's go hit some houses in the city. We'll kick in the doors. If there's anybody home, we'll tie them up. We'll take everything they've got and go make some money. Are you down for it?"

I said, "I'm down for whatever."

There was nothing they could have suggested that I would not have agreed to because I didn't care. It felt like I had a risk gene in me that loved taking a dangerous gamble. Today, it still shows up through scenarios where I trust God for big things, but there is no danger, only the excitement that comes from serving God. Back then, however, the scarier it was, the better. We went on our spree from 10 AM to 3 PM, kicking in doors and taking whatever we wanted. Thankfully, there was never anybody home, so we didn't hurt anybody, but we certainly shattered their privacy when we invaded. We went from house to house and around 3 PM, we decided to hit one last house and call it a day.

I will never forget walking up to that last front door. I thought, *Something is going to go wrong.* I should have felt that at 10 AM but didn't, but at 3 PM, I did but ignored the thought. The girl who was with us was driving the getaway car and was prepared to do whatever we needed, so I thought, *We're good.* We kicked in the front door and, once in the house, started pulling things off the wall and grabbing anything of value. This house was going to make our whole day worthwhile.

We were pulling things together to leave when I looked out the window and saw a police car pulling up in front of our getaway car. The police officer took the girl out of the driver's seat and put her in the back seat of the police car. We panicked and knew we had to get out of there. I had handed my gun to my friend but he got scared and handed it back to me. I took it and broke out the side window in the house, dove out of the window, hit the ground, and started running through yards on the northwest side of Oklahoma City.

As I was fleeing, blood was running down my arm from the broken glass, but I still had the gun in my hand. As I looked down the street on my right, there was an unmarked police car coming to a screeching halt. A plainclothes officer jumped out of the vehicle and drew his weapon, resting his arm on the roof of the vehicle. We were about 20 feet away from one another when he yelled, "Drop your weapon!"

I was wired and had an adrenaline-rush reaction. I raised my weapon toward him, charging him and screaming, "You drop your weapon or I'm going to shoot." Before I could squeeze the trigger, I heard five or six pops ring out, sounding like bottle rockets, and I saw smoke filling the air. It felt like a sledgehammer hit me in the chest and the bullets flung me around while everything seemed to unfold in slow motion. I was hit in my chest, arm, and hand.

Things began to glow and I could sense and even see every molecule in the air. I knew I hit the ground, but it felt like a cloud. I was lying there and I heard a ringing in my head. I was looking around wondering what had just happened. I slowly started to feel things come back into focus.

The weather was clear and nice as a spring day, but I sensed strange wetness on my face like spring rain. When I looked down at my chest, I saw there was a red liquid squirting from it. A bullet had severed one of my arteries and blood was spurting out of my chest all over the place. That was the rain. Before long, I was lying in a pool of my blood, and I started to get cold.

There were so many things happening at once. I could hear everything, including my friends, running, trying to get away from the officers. I heard the expletives they were screaming at the police. The police officer who shot me was kneeling next to me to make sure I wasn't going anywhere. I could see his head turning, looking left and right to ensure that he was safe and secure.

Then I saw the ambulance come. The medic was holding my chest while they lifted me and put me in. Those in the ambulance frantically worked on me. There were all kinds of unfamiliar noises in the ambulance. The machinery kept beeping, the medics sounded like they were shouting, and then things went black. When I regained consciousness, it felt like I had been shocked by something. I lost all vital signs for about 20 seconds and 65% of my blood supply had left my body. By God's grace, the paramedics preserved my life and brought me back.

We arrived at Baptist Medical Center where they took me into the prep room for surgery. They cut off my clothes and an eight ball of cocaine fell out of my pocket onto the floor, landing next to a police officer's foot. I thought to myself, *Well, that's just icing on the cake*. Then I blacked out again.

When I woke up, I was in the Intensive Care Unit, handcuffed to a bed. I thought, *Wow! What just happened? The day started with a plan to make some money, kick in some doors, and hit some houses. How did I end up here?* I had no idea how seriously I had been injured and I spent the rest of that day clinging to life. I was left alone with God and my thoughts, wondering what would happen next and what all this meant for me. I had tried to kill a police officer and I was in serious trouble if I survived my wounds.

The next time I woke up, I was in a special room, still at the Baptist Medical Center. Sitting in my room was a white man in his mid- to late-thirties who was a plainclothes policeman. He impressed me as kind and he was smiling at me—not agitated or combative even though I had murderous thoughts toward his colleagues. He spoke first and to my surprise said, "Glad to see you're still with us," or something to that effect. I was a heavy smoker at the time and would have given my arm for a smoke, so I asked him if there was any way he could give me one, adding, "It's been a rough day." He said he was not permitted to do that, but even his refusal was kind.

I was in the hospital for two weeks. As soon as I could sit up in the bed, they informed me that it was time for me to go to the county jail. Therefore, at 18 years of age, while high on pain meds, dressed in a paper gown, with my hand, mangled and wrapped, and barely able to walk, the police took me off to jail. My life would never be the same.

CHAPTER FOUR

Prison Life

They put me on a bus and once there, the jailers took me to the fourth floor, which was the felony floor at the time. When asked to share my story, I joke and say that the county jail was so bad that even the cockroaches only do drive-bys. It was an old, drab facility with gray bars, and I have never been able to describe the smell, one that I still can't get out of my mind. It's the odor of hopelessness where living human beings are warehoused for their crimes as they await trial. Believe me when I tell you that the jail was an awful place.

I was a mess when I arrived. I weighed about 105 pounds and I was a broken, dysfunctional human being. The fourth floor had side cells with four bunks. In my cell, there were already five people, one in each bunk. There was one guy on the floor so they put me on the floor near the toilet. The jailer made a comment that he thought was funny when he brought me in, saying, "This white boy tried to shoot the Po Po (slang for police)."

What he didn't realize was that his comment piqued their interest in me and gave me instant street credibility with my new friends. They would say, "We heard what happened to you. Did you try to shoot the police? What happened?" and they listened sympathetically—some even admired me. It may sound strange, but the Lord used that as a form of protection, for the men felt they needed to take care of me since I had struck a blow against those who they perceived to be our common enemy: the police. One said, "Get this man a blanket." Another shouted an order to no one in particular, "Someone grab him some cookies. Take care of him." They rallied around me and gave me one of the bunks. Thankfully, about four hours later, my brother Joey showed up and posted bond to get me out, using the money my mom had pulled together and given him.

I should have been relieved to be out of jail, but I didn't have a clue what to do from here. I could not use my left arm. I was weak, confused, and facing a dark and uncertain future. My girlfriend met me at my brother's house, where I stayed for the next eight months. As if I wasn't in enough trouble, she got pregnant almost immediately after I got out. Those eight months constitute the deepest and darkest period in my life. I spiraled even deeper into drug addiction by popping pain pills and anything else I could get my hands on. There were days when I would be up all night wired up on meth.

I would take 10 to 20 valium a day to calm my nerves, then I would pass out. I tried any kind of drug I could get my hands on. I even tried to sell drugs during that time, but people wanted nothing to do with me. After eight months, I had to go back to the county jail. I entered a blind guilty plea, which means there is no bargaining for a length of sentence. It is strictly up to the discretion of the judge. After I entered that plea, I had to spend a month in the county jail while they evaluated me.

Two weeks later, they took me from the county jail, shackled in chains and dressed in an orange jumpsuit, over to the courthouse. As I walked into the courtroom, I saw my girlfriend in the lobby pointing to her stomach, trying to tell me her water had broken and she was in labor. My entire family was present for my hearing. Distracted by my girlfriend in labor, I was forced to face the sentencing of the court. I approached the judge having no idea what was going to happen. I gave my best appeal for mercy, but the judge was not moved. He sentenced me to 47 years in prison. At 18 years of age, I thought my life was over. That's when I broke. I was angry at God, thinking all this was His fault because He took my father from me. I had made God the focus of my anger.

At that moment, I realized I had believed a lie. I was the only person to blame for my current mess. I was angry my father had been taken out of my life and now my criminal behavior ensured that I, too, would be taken out of my baby's life. That wasn't God's fault;

it was mine. After my sentence, I went back to the county jail, got on my face in my cell, and repented. I asked God to forgive me, praying, "If there's anything left, if there are any brain cells left in my head, they are Yours to use."

One of the first things I did was to write letters to people whom I hurt, asking for their forgiveness. That was the beginning of a season of transformation when God grew me into the leader He wanted me to be, first in that county jail and then in prison. I miraculously ended up serving only eight calendar years because of good behavior. It all began in the county jail cell on my face, crying out to God. He radically took hold of my life at that moment.

While I yielded my life to the Lord in my cell after sentencing, there was still denial that all this was happening to me. I expected to find some loophole allowing me to get out early, and that sense lasted for about one year before the harsh reality set in—I was going to spend an indefinite amount of time in prison.

I stepped into those confined spaces with double razor-wire fencing, iron bars, slamming gates, and unsavory characters, and prison became my school where I was spiritually developed and formed. As I look back, I know my emotional and spiritual development was stunted because of the bitterness, anger, and rage gripping my heart, along with my drug use and abuse. I had to be stripped of everything I had known of who I was before I went to prison. At first, I was always on alert: What's going to happen to me? I had heard so many stories about prison, and I wasn't looking forward to new ones featuring me cast in the lead role.

During my first year in prison, I gravitated toward and hung around with people who were a positive influence and were trying to do the right things. I regularly ran into old friends and former acquaintances who were not trying to do the right thing. They respected the fact that my life was changing, however, and as I stated earlier, they respected what brought me to prison in the first place. I had respect on both sides of the fence—those who were walking in newness of life and those who were still fighting the system and saw me as someone who was fighting too—and God used them all to protect me and help me grow.

I started my incarceration journey doing good time, earning time off for good behavior by enrolling in life-skills or drug-rehabilitation programs. The first facility I went to was Lexington, an assessment and receiving facility, where I stayed until all my testing was done. Then I went on to James Crabtree Correctional Facility in Helena, Oklahoma, my first experience in a high-to-medium-level security facility. Men there were lifers, drug traffickers, rapists, killers, and some of the worst of the worst, all housed in a military-style, open-door, bunk-bed facility.

I shipped in from Lexington to Crabtree at about 3 AM, crawling quietly into the top bunk of a unit, realizing I was in an open-dorm prison where anything can happen to anyone. There was only one guard and he was about 50 feet away from me. I was afraid but at the same time, I had a sense of peace thinking, Here I am, God. Walk before me and with me in this process. I was determined to do whatever He had for me to do so I could become a better person.

It blows my mind how God completely protected

me my entire time in prison. I did not get into one fight or even experience one situation where I was in a violent altercation. This was not an easy task. I was in several Oklahoma prisons that had reputations for violence and disorder. Word had gotten around that I had attempted to shoot a police officer. The reputation of my crime gave me major street 'cred' and kept me out of trouble. The relationships I had before prison with diverse gang members helped too.

I had relationships and respect on both the black and white side of gang affiliation in prison, which is not common in that environment. I even had respect from the Latino contingent. I had respect in all circles, and honestly, it wasn't anything I earned other than how I carried myself in the yard, what I stood for, but also what I used to stand for. It was an odd collaboration of favor and influence.

Don't get me wrong. There were scary times during my eight years in prison. One of my earliest scares happened when I was in my first prison at the James Crabtree Facility, an old building that formerly housed a boy's reformatory before being converted into a men's prison. As I mentioned, this facility was an open-dorm facility, which meant it was also open showering. I had been in two months when an older inmate came in while I was taking a shower. He was known on the yard as a "buzzard"—somebody who sexually preyed on younger people coming into prison.

By then, I probably weighed 120 pounds soaking wet. I was not too far removed from being shot and recovering from bad drug addiction. I was weak and pretty much defenseless if someone was going to attack me. He came in and took the shower spot right next to me, talking to me while looking at me suggestively. I thought, All right. Here's what I've seen in the movies and heard about. I don't know what's going to happen, but I am going to go down in flames if I must. I was going to come out swinging. In the end, only one of us will be standing.

My thoughts were interrupted by three big gangbangers who knew me from the street They said, "No way," and blocked the guy who was in the shower with me and told him in no uncertain terms he was not taking a shower there with me. They said, "This guy's one of us. He's off limits to you." I saw God's protection at that moment.

When a man (or woman) is in that environment, it is normal to see a little bit of violence here and there. Once there was a huge riot on the yard when inmates in a lockdown unit somehow knocked out the guard who was overseeing them. They broke loose and spread all over the yard. I saw several people get stabbed and saw others hit in the head with barbells and other objects. Violence was all around me, but I clung to my faith believing God had a hopeful future for me beyond these walls.

Every man was out to protect himself and no one knew where loyalties might lie. Inmates took the opportunity to target someone who owed them money or who was of a different race. Once, I retreated to a corner during a riot and heard people run by me, saying, "Oh, it's Jed. He's not in on this. He's not part of this," and move on. It was God's sovereign protection. It didn't take long before the prison SWAT team came in to shut it all down. It was a minor riot by prison standards, but it was still a riot. I didn't want to be part of it. I was trying to go home and get to my son. Although it eventually blew over, the shock of it all remained.

On another occasion, I witnessed a man get stabbed twelve times while standing only three people in front of me in the commissary line. Everyone looked away and acted like it was not happening and hoped it didn't come into their space. If we were asked questions about what happened, we played dumb. That's how everyone survived and stayed out of trouble, but I wasn't just anybody—I was God's child and He was protecting me. I don't want you to think that there were not positive moments in prison, because there were. I had many encounters with inmates whom God used to shape and mold me.

CHAPTER FIVE

Hope

I could relate more prison horror stories, but as I write, I find it difficult to remember many of them, although I know they are in my memory banks if I probed more deeply. For my entire time served, I stayed focused on the good God wanted to do in my life to prepare me for my release—and He had a lot of work to do. I also don't want this book to merely highlight the tragic events of my journey—there is so much good that God weaved into my time in prison.

I was in a program called the Therapeutic Community at the Davis Correctional Facility where I served time in 1998. It was a live-in-community recovery program and it was touted as a program that prepared inmates to get out of prison. I genuinely wanted to be a part of it, not to help me be released early, but because I always felt I had leadership in me and if possible, I wanted to be part of that Community to help me recognize and develop what was in me.

We had an exercise in the Community called the Relation Chair, which required that we sit down in a chair facing another person and talk to that person for five hours a week. We had to get to know each other's culture, history, weaknesses, strengths, regrets, and other intimate details. I can still see myself sitting in that chair, and it was my favorite part of the program because God used that exercise to develop my love of hearing other people's stories. That practice made me a better listener and developed more empathy for the pain others were experiencing.

I grew up in the Church of Christ, which is quite traditional with hymnals but no children's Sunday School in the version of which we were a part. All the children were in the same room with the family for the Sunday School teaching. Then we went into the main church service with the pastor behind the pulpit. When I came to prison, I began attending chapel services where we had a variety of volunteers who came from many different denominations and ministry expressions.

It was interesting because I had not been exposed to Spirit-filled churches, people who spoke in tongues, or other expressions of faith. Some volunteers came in and just "blew my hair back," as they preached loud and long, and then prayed for people, expecting that we would be moved by the Spirit and fall under His power. I was not accustomed to that style of ministry, but I sensed some of those folks were genuine and authentic.

There is an empowerment that comes with knowing Jesus and allowing the Spirit to flow through us and guide us in this life. There were a few, and I can't remember their names or the names of their churches, who had that balance of God the Father, God the Son, and God the Holy Spirit, showing us how they work together to provide the guidance and strength to do what God has called us to do. That became real to me and it made a lot of sense.

I was filled with the Holy Spirit in prison and that was a significant moment, but I didn't fall on the floor or start shouting as some people believe should accompany that experience. I don't believe the only evidence of the baptism in the Spirit is when someone speaks in tongues. After my born-again experience in the county jail, I went through various stages of development as a Christ-follower, and one stage was when I knew I was filled with the Holy Spirit. I began sensing the Spirit lead me much more often than before. I responded by connecting with certain people and participating in certain programs. When I felt led to share my faith with people, I would observe how my obedience to the leading of the Spirit led to God being present in my conversations. I heard men say, "Nobody ever asked if they could pray for me. Yes, please pray."

There were significant moments throughout my time when I had deep conversations with some tough, calloused convicts. I probably had three or four different guys who are out and have found me on Facebook to say, "I just want you to know that it may have seemed like I wasn't listening to you in prison, but I accepted Jesus at some point. I trace it back to conversations we had just sitting on the line. You weren't trying to convert me, but you were just talking about your faith and how it played out in your life."

Those encounters were always special when I saw the Holy Spirit at work in people's lives. I learned all I had to do was show up and love people, and I have seen that as a pattern in my life. I have never felt like I had to push my faith on anyone; it's always been my way to build relationships and allow the Holy Spirit room to work in the hearts of people and reveal the love of Christ.

While in prison, for example, we used to play this game called casino and I played it every day with a man who was in for murder. This man was outspoken and angry. At one time, he was a Satanist but when we met, he was an atheist. We played casino every day and talked about everything and anything while we played. If led by the Holy Spirit, I would often ask questions he might have considered intrusive, but he would usually respond positively to my questions. It was fascinating to see this guy, who was so angry and had built fences, walls, and barriers around himself, open up a little bit at a time.

I worked to build a relationship with him and I saw the walls come down. This was the kind of stuff that built my faith in the future. All the time, I prayed, "God, I know You have something for me. I'm praying for my wife. I am praying for my purpose. I hope to do something great whenever I get out of prison." I kept stirring my faith and thinking, *I know there's something greater beyond this.*

I still find it difficult to remember specific things from those years. I was putting in my time and focusing on getting out, so I blocked out a lot that happened, even the good things, for as much as God was doing and protecting me, I was still traumatized. I was terrified of some of my fellow inmates who had serious problems and appeared to be ticking time bombs waiting to explode. I hoped and prayed they would not be around me when they went off.

There was one significant moment that stands out from the rest as I approached the time for my release. By then, I had four guys who became lifelong friends. Two of them are out of prison now and living successful lives. We were in Taft, Oklahoma at the Jess Dunn Correctional Center. Taft was a minimum-security facility, so it was the first time I could go outside the fence and walk around freely. There was a special unit for inmates located outside the compound fence, and we had special jobs.

Every night we would go to what we called the upper room. It was the second level of this unit, a little tucked-away space where we sat, talked, and prayed. We would talk about our dreams: "Let's pray for the wife God has for us. Let's pray for what He would have us do outside this fence. Let's pray for the people in our unit." We grew to be quite close.

I look back at those prayers now and I marvel, *God, You were listening and answered all those prayers.* I specifically prayed for the wife I have today. Julie is a godly woman and we serve side-by-side as we oversee City Center (much more on her later). I prayed for a specific ministry: "God, I want to impact kids like me. I want to impact youth who have great challenges before them." Here we are today seeing those prayers also being answered.

I fervently prayed, "Lord, preserve the relationship with my son," and sure enough, He has preserved it. I see God's faithfulness when I look back and see myself in that hopeless situation. I was surrounded by people who were totally broken and mentally ill, with all kinds of problems and personality disorders. The only thing I had to cling to was my faith and the hope there was a future for me. There was and is a future and a hope and I'm living them today. I consider that a powerful testimony.

Now that I am out, I'm reading and learning more about trauma and Post-Traumatic Stress Syndrome. I recently read a book called *The Body Keeps a Score*. In a Christian worldview, some expect all the trauma and negative residue to be wiped away once someone accepts Jesus and is born-again. The thinking is that we shouldn't have to go back and deal with these things, seeking healing from the past. That's not been my experience because I have met many people who accepted Christ but felt like something was wrong with them because they were still struggling with anxiety, fear, or some other disorder. As I have been on this journey the last few years, I recognize that I encountered some serious trauma and it has had an effect on me—and still does to this day.

When I think of it, the list is significant. I was shot. I was in prison. I have seen people stabbed and beaten, even before prison. I was shot at several times and shot at people several times. I lost my dad at a young age. I saw my brother abuse my mom after my dad passed away. I remember seeing violent altercations between my brothers. My mom had her hands full trying to provide for us after she spent months caring for my dad when he had cancer.

God has healed me—a former criminal and now a functioning citizen who is adding value to my community rather than stripping it of resources for my gain. I have learned how to hear God's voice and obey the leading of the Holy Spirit, but there is still stuff that returns—pictures of my past, words that were spoken, memories of the pain. I wonder if this is what the apostle Paul meant by his "thorn in the flesh"? Some of that stuff lingers for a reason. We identify with Christ the most in our pain and some of my painful memories help maintain a high level of empathy and compassion, and dependence upon Him.

Some people I was housed with will probably never get out of prison, but I always knew my time would end and I would be a free man. Before I tell you about my release, let me share about my family and how God used my time in prison to bring healing and reconciliation.

CHAPTER SIX

My Angel

My newborn son and girlfriend helped motivate me to do good when I first entered prison. I wanted to be a better husband (we got married once I was in prison) and father, and I knew I had to do what I needed to do. As the years behind bars added up, it became difficult for my girlfriend and then wife to hang on and hang in as a young mother with our son. After a while, she quit coming to see me but continued to make sure my son and I had visits through my mom. My mom was faithful to come to visit once and some-times twice a month, driving six hours from Texas to

Oklahoma and back again. It may sound strange, but my time of imprisonment helped strengthen my relationship with my son, mom, and family. We had opportunities for reconciliation and healing on different levels throughout my time in prison.

During my eight years of incarceration, I found it particularly challenging to deal with the failure of my marriage to my son's mother. It was extremely painful for me to see that my choices caused her pain and difficulty. Let me be clear: My son's mother is not to blame for the failure of our marriage. She was a young mom doing an incredible job raising a young man on her own and she needed to do what was best for her and our son while I was away serving time. She responded to the circumstances she was given.

I did learn, however, that we identify more closely with Christ in our pain than in our victories and blessings. Whenever we experience hurt and pain, we are propelled into our greatest moments of growth and understanding. In my pain, I learned to welcome and embrace other types of suffering as opportunities to grow and identify with Jesus. I moved from one prison yard to another after I became involved in a work program in which I was on an asbestos removal crew. I spent seven years and seven months in prison being as productive as I could be—because I wanted to get out and watch my son grow up.

My son's name is Jedidiah Angel Carole Chappell. He was a beacon of hope for me whenever he was born and whenever he would come see me. I was moved by how much he loved me and how proud he was of me, which was remarkable considering my situation. He looks so much like me and we share many characteristics. The facilities where I was housed had little space for visitors, especially children. In the beginning, I was always excited to have him there. We would play, and he was oblivious to everything going on in and outside the room.

We would sit down when he first arrived and pray—me first and then him. Then my mom would pray. We would read Scriptures and talk about what he thought they meant. He had a young, innocent faith that was developing early on. There was one time where I walked him through the Lord's Prayer and the sinner's prayer, and he accepted Jesus into his heart. That was closer to when he was six years old, but it was quite genuine and real. We talked about that decision and what it meant.

We had a great relationship, and as time progressed and I moved from medium-security to minimum-security prisons, we were able to play outside and spend more time together. He was the driving motivation, outside of my relationship with Jesus, to get out of prison and be successful. To me, my picture of success was having any job that would enable me to bring home a check every week. I was determined to reenter civilian life and be responsible.

I was on the bottom bunk most of the time during my eight years. Whenever I looked up, I saw the pictures I had placed underneath the top bunk of my family—most of which were of my son, who we often referred to as Angel. I would lay on my back, touching those pictures and praying God would protect, guard, and keep him, and that He would preserve our relationship. I quoted Bible verses and promises over those pictures, honing in on Angel's spiritual formation.

Eventually, it became more challenging when he had to go home or when our time was limited. He didn't understand why he had to go or why there were so many restrictions. There were even rules and regulations about how long I could hold him on my lap. Overall, those moments when I had him with his mom or my mom in the visiting room were powerful motivators to keep me focused on getting out.

When I was released, my mom, niece, and nephew came to pick me up from Jackie Brennan Correctional Facility in McAllister, Oklahoma. I had made parole, but it took 30 to 90 days before they finally approved it. I got word the governor was going to sign my parole, but I would not know the exact day. About 60 days later, a guard informed me I should have my stuff together in the morning because I would be shipping out. He did not say if I would be going home or going to another facility. He had this look on his face and a sly smile and he liked me, so I concluded, *I'm going home tomorrow.*

I had a serious case of butterflies in my gut. I was not anxious or scared, but it was excitement welling up within me. When my mom came, first they took me into a room and gave me a package that had some new clothes from Gap. I said to myself, *These are real street clothes. These are not blue jeans and a shirt made by the State.* They didn't completely fit the way I would have liked, but these were brand-new clothes, not prison clothes. I distinctly remember that they smelled like a department store.

Then I walked through the gates and saw my mom and family in their minivan. They came up and hugged me, and I knew I was out of prison. I got in the van and we drove away. Like most prisons, it was in a remote rural area, but I was finally breathing the fresh air of a free man. I saw all the trees, fence posts, and mile markers going by quickly. My mom was playing an album by the group Third Day.

The first place she took me was Walmart to get some hygiene products. In hindsight, that was not a good idea. In prison, there is an unofficial three-feet rule. No one can enter or violate anyone's three feet of space by walking too close or touching anyone. I lived a God-honoring life in prison, but there were effects from being institutionalized that impacted me—and I didn't even realize it. As a result, when people bumped into me in Walmart, I thought they were being disrespectful. My anxiety escalated quickly, and I had to get out of there. There was too much to take in at one time.

The day after I got out, I went to pick my son up from school. This was the moment I was finally able to be part of his life. I lost my dad early in life and missed the fatherly direction I wanted or needed. This was my shot at getting it right with my son. Angel was almost eight years old and attending Sequoia School. I arrived in my mom's van wearing sweatpants and a t-shirt with tennis shoes.

We had notified the school ahead of time that I was going to pick him up instead of his mom, and the principal knew my whole story. As I stood in the school lobby, the kids lined up to get picked up by their parents in the drive-through area. I saw Angel's big brown eyes light up when he saw me. He jumped up and down, raising his hand to catch the teacher's eye while being quiet and respectful. He said, "That's my dad. That's my dad," and then took off running, jumping into my arms. This was the moment we both had dreamed about. I felt every part of his embrace as if it was the first time to hold my son. The park would be our next destination.

Angel's mom has always been supportive of me being involved in his life. For me, this was God's promise being fulfilled. One of my biggest fears was that he wouldn't want to be around me or he'd be embarrassed by me. It was humorous that he would simply tell his friends, "My dad just got out of prison," and then talk about how proud he was of me.

Little did I know that the concept of this book began unfolding during my reunion with my son. My relationship with him had begun when I was being taken into court for sentencing and his mother's water broke in the lobby. I developed and maintained a relationship with him during my prison years and when I picked him up at school, I had come full circle—or I should say God had brought me full circle to be a part of his life. This pattern was repeated in the years following my release and is still playing out as I write. God continues to demonstrate that He is truly a *Full-Circle God*.

CHAPTER SEVEN

"God, Show Me The One."

I was released on May 7, 2003, delighted, but facing questions I had never confronted before: *What are my next steps? Where will I work? Where will I live?* I had never held a job, and my only experience was selling drugs and performing other illegal activities to make money. I had learned that integrity could take me a long way, farther than being a criminal ever could—now I had to prove that to be true.

My reunion with my son had gone well, and that

was a great relief to me. After that, I began to settle into life in the real world—joining a church, finding a job, and establishing a new rhythm and a new normal. It was a challenge because the only place I had to live once I got out was with a family member in a challenging environment. I was on parole, so I could not afford to make any mistakes and I was determined to do whatever I had to do to make it and move on with my life. My efforts were rewarded when my parole officer released me from parole status, acknowledging what a great job I was doing. Not too long after that, I got my place to live and someone gave me a car.

I knew one thing: My mother, father, and brothers worked hard, and I wanted to do the same. I had worked hard as a drug dealer, and in prison, I worked diligently at multiple jobs. I didn't have a problem re-entering the workforce, for my work ethic was the equal of the rest of my family. When I sought employment, I was always open and transparent with employers about my past, explaining what I had done. Whatever they needed me to do to ensure a safe workspace for them, I was happy to do. I wanted them to know I would be the hardest worker they had ever had. I was always able to quickly connect with most people because I knew how to look for and build on common ground. I had developed good relational skills in prison through the Relation Chair, and I found I could quickly win over employers despite my troublesome past.

God gave me a high level of self-awareness when I got out. I struggled at times with the issue of others disrespecting me—a big issue in the prison world. I prayed, "Lord, help me navigate truth and not be influenced by my experiences in prison. Help me to recognize the difference between what's true and what I learned by being conditioned in the prison environment I had lived in." God was always faithful to help me and once again answered my prayer. It's humbling to look back and see how the Holy Spirit was working in my life.

My first task was to find employment as a former convict. I started landscaping with one of my brothers and eventually took a catering job. I got up early in the morning and did prep cooking for the caterers and set up the rooms. I worked hard to climb the ladder and to prove I was valuable. I knew if I could learn everything people did wherever I worked, then I knew I would become a valued employee and teammate. I would lie awake at night, reviewing the details of the day, retracing every task, and wondering if I had done enough. My hard work paid off and, through one relationship after another, I began to secure better jobs and eventually finished my college degree at a local community college in computer-aided design. This led to a short career in video editing and producing. Then, I found the job that changed my career path. I jumped into my first ministry job at the City Rescue Mission, a local homeless shelter.

I started attending Victory Church in Oklahoma City soon after I got out of prison. It was there that I met my wife, Julie. I didn't want to waste time dating, so I prayed for God to bring someone to walk beside me. On Wednesday night, a pastor by the name of Craig Groeschel was speaking at Victory on relationships. We reached the point in the service when we were to turn and greet someone near us. I saw her in the row in front of me but ten people over. We caught each other's attention and both stretched out to greet each other, but it was obvious we were too far away. Although the moment was awkward, I was deeply impacted by our brief connection, and I couldn't shake the thought, *God is she the one?*

In an attempt to create an unlikely scenario that I would run into her again, I planned to go to a different Sunday church service than I would normally attend. *If she's the one, God, create a situation where we engage in conversation and I don't have to make any effort for it to happen.* Sure enough, God was guiding our steps.

On the following Sunday, we found ourselves alone in the lobby, normally a very crowded space. We struck up a conversation as we entered the auditorium. Angel and I sat down on one side, Julie on the other. Angel asked, "Dad, why don't we go over and sit next to her?" His question challenged me to take the step that would begin my journey with Julie. I asked if we could join her, and she said yes!

We would talk every Sunday and Wednesday at church, and then one night she suggested, "Why don't you come over to my apartment for coffee some night? I have my boys there and you can bring Angel." We accepted and that was our first official date. She told me her life story and it was obvious we had very different experiences. She felt she was a terrible person because she would have an adult beverage every once in a while.

I thought, *Oh man! She's going to collapse when she hears my story.* I got increasingly nervous as she wrapped up her squeaky clean story. I knew it was my turn next. "So tell me your story," she prompted. I was crippled with fear and anxiety as the words came out of her mouth. When they did, I took a deep breath and poured out my whole story. She looked like a deer in the headlights for about five minutes, but then said, "It's great to see how God has transformed your life." I was sure I had ruined any chance of a future relationship with her, but she affirmed that I was not my past and said it with eyes that were sincere and free of any judgment or disappointment.

Later she told me that she felt peace by reframing my story and thinking, *That was his past and we are in his present, and God has his future*. After that, we began to date and hang out more and more, although we didn't hold hands or kiss for several weeks. She now tells me she wondered whether I liked or cared about her, or if I even liked women.

We went out to dinner at Lake Hefner for an official date and after dinner, sat on a wall and looked out over the lake. I felt like I was supposed to make my move respectfully, but I remember being paralyzed by fear. She said, "You know, I like you and I wouldn't be offended if you wanted to hold my hand." She was leading me which caused me to lock up even more.

I said, "Okay, thanks," but it was super awkward. When I didn't respond, she had a disappointed and confused look on her face. We started to walk back to the car and I was saying to myself, *Man, you've just blown your chance. You should've had more courage. She's going to think you're lunatic or something.* Then I felt like the *Eye of the Tiger* theme from Rocky started playing in my head and I said to myself, *I'm going to go ahead and make a move.*

We got close to the car, I finally got up the courage and grabbed her hand and kissed her. She said, "Thank you so much! I was worried you weren't interested in me." I looked over and we were standing next to a nasty, disgusting, stinky, trash-filled garbage can. I thought, *Way to go, Jed. You finally get up the courage to give her the first kiss and you're standing by a garbage can.* We quickly knew we were to be married because we had a deep affection for the Lord and one another. When I eventually proposed to her, we were standing next to a dumpster. We got married in 2003, and I'm happy to report that our wedding took place without the presence of trash receptacles.

Julie and I work side-by-side at City Center, where she operates in the COO role. She deals with systems and logistics, finance, and oversees the staff. Before City Center, she worked as an occupational therapist. When I met her, she was a single mom with two boys, recently divorced, and putting herself through college to become an occupational therapist. She would later make the difficult decision to step away from her lucrative career to serve full-time at the City Center.

The kids at the City Center call her Momma Julie. She has an amazing ability to cut through the layers of protection and anger that have been built around so many of our kids and speak straight to their hearts. God has used both her past experiences and her professional training to be such a strength to our City Center team. I watch in amazement as our hardest kids melt when she puts her arm around them.

Although Julie was forgiving of my past, she was concerned about her dad's reaction. She had hoped to wait until after we got married to share it with him, but I insisted he needed to know about me *before* we got married. I knew she was an adult and had no obligation to get his permission, but I felt it was prudent to fill him in as early as possible. Julie's dad is a retired Marine Corps veteran helicopter gunner. He was shot down, broke his back, and was in a coma for a week or two. I had great respect for him and wanted to honor him in this way.

For the first eight months, we were dating, he didn't know anything about me. I had already proposed and the wedding date was set before I had the opportunity to inform her parents of my past. We decided to do it and went over to his house without a plan of what we were going to say or how we are going to bring it up. We walked into their house without a plan but determined to bring it up. I made small talk. I told him that the wedding was getting expensive. Julie's dad responded that we were young and suggested we should rob a bank.

Out of the blue, Julie said, "Oh, by the way, Dad, Jed was in prison for eight years." He responded, "Well, people can change. What were you in for?" I said, "Well, you know, just drugs and being a dumb kid," trying to minimize the seriousness of what I had done. I couldn't believe she threw me under the bus like that! After we got married, her dad asked me about the specifics of what happened, so we sat down and I walked him through everything. He was accepting of me and didn't make any judgments.

Her stepmom is who she calls Mom now. Her mom passed away from lung cancer when she was about 18. Julie shared with me that her mom had battled mental illness and, for that reason, was more of a friend than a parent. At the age of 18, she sat by her mom's side and held her hand as she died. Although she was angry with God, she made a vow that she would not be weak. She was determined not to feel the same pain her mom did. She found herself alone and unprepared to deal with life. Her pain, however, caused her to be even more intentional to be a good mom. We had more in common than I had previously thought. Julie and I both lost the same-sex parent to the same disease. Our paths were strangely similar after all.

Today, we have four boys—his, hers, and ours. Our oldest is my boy Angel from my previous marriage. We have Julie's two boys, Conner and Kyler, from her previous marriage, and then our boy, Jaxon, who is 13. We are a blended family that has figured out how to make it work, and we have a civil relationship with the other families.

As I write, I look around at our quiet home and realize that our boys are now men. Angel is currently working at a restaurant. Conner is 21 and he's working as an HVAC maintenance man while pursuing his journeyman's license to work in that field. Kyler is 19 and graduated from Fort Benning Army Airborne. Currently, he is stationed at Fort Hood in Austin. Jaxon is 13 and still at home with us. They are all quite smart, but Jaxon is wise beyond his years. We have nicknamed him the old man. He's attending eighth grade, loving school, and doing well there. I am so proud of who my boys have become. At times, I struggle with the pain of regret when I think of how my choices might have negatively impacted them, but I am amazed at how God redeemed my broken past. I am thankful that my family is so close.

Not only had I prayed for a wife while I was in prison, I asked God to use me any way He saw fit. I wanted to reach the lost, and I knew I could reach people just like I had been doing in prison. Little did I know that God had been listening and would answer that prayer in ways I never could have imagined.

CHAPTER EIGHT

"Me? A Pastor?"

I had been attending Victory Church only a few weeks when the youth pastor took notice of me. They needed volunteers whose responsibilities on Sundays were to greet people and shake as many hands as possible. He and I spoke on several occasions and then one Sunday, he surprised me when he said, "You know, you would be an incredible youth volunteer," to which I responded, "You should do a background check, hear my story, and learn about my past before you try to make that happen!"

Despite how opposite our pasts had been, there

was strong chemistry between us. I'm almost certain he said the Lord's Prayer in his mother's womb, while I was the guy who spent eight years in prison. The youth pastor laughed when I told him my whole story. At first, he was taken aback but quickly embraced who I was and I started to volunteer. The youth group at the time was a diverse and challenging collection of teens with a lot of at-risk young people. I threw myself into my role on the team and volunteered to help whenever I could.

This was a special time because it was my first volunteer experience in a church. At that time, the Victory Church youth group met in a building across the street from today's main campus. Now it's the building we own at City Center, using it to serve hundreds of local youth every week. It's crazy to see how God gave us ownership of the very building where I began my ministry as a volunteer!

As a volunteer, I became closer with other staff members, especially the worship leader and his wife, who supervised all the adult ministries. We would talk often and he would tell me that he thought I should be a pastor. Then there was an open position at the church for a small group director. He asked if I would be willing to talk to his wife about that position. I was surprised because I thought I would work in the maintenance department or maybe as a janitor. I was not thinking I would be considered for a ministry position.

I continued to feel unqualified and disqualified for the position. I thought it was crazy I was even having an interview. Shortly into the interview, his wife stopped and apologized, "I'm so sorry. I have such a terrible migraine. I'm going to have to cut this interview short." I thought it was her way of saying I wasn't the man for the job. I understood if she saw red flags and needed a quick out. A week later, she called and offered me the position.

My wife and I talked about it and decided I should take the position, so I became the leader of the small group ministry at Victory Church under Hillary Grantham. At my first staff meeting, the senior pastor went on stage and introduced me, handed me a microphone, and asked me to tell my story—putting me on the spot in front of 75 people in the room and a larger streaming audience.

The whole staff embraced me and my story. Pastor Mark, then the lead pastor, proceeded to say not only was I going to lead the small groups, but I was going to lead the biggest outreach initiative the church had ever conducted called the Order of the Towel. At that moment, a big outreach ministry was born that I was supposed to lead. I had no idea what was ahead.

The next Sunday, Pastor Mark delivered an amazing sermon about how Jesus came to serve and not be served. He promised we were going to reach outside the church walls. We were going to pick up our towel and figuratively wash the feet of the city— thus the name the Order of the Towel. Six hundred people signed up to help after his message. I was responsible to contact, train, and lead all of these volunteers to demonstrate the love of Christ to our city.

I had no ministry experience, had only been out of prison for four years, and had no clue as to where to begin. Before I knew it, I had the privilege of leading 600 volunteers doing monthly, quarterly, and weekly outreaches in the broken communities in Oklahoma City, the very communities I helped to poison as a drug dealer. We started in 2007 and gained momentum in 2008. I started in those areas as a sinner but was now returning to serve the sinner.

I was working at the catering service with Julie before I came on staff at the church. I joined the Victory Church staff in July 2007 as Small Groups and Outreach Director. About 60 days into my service there, they assigned me the title of pastor. At that time, they had never promoted someone from a director to be a pastor.

I suddenly found myself a staff pastor at a church of about 8,000 members. The pastor began promising even bigger results from this new, outreach effort. I felt intense pressure to perform in an arena for which I felt completely ill-equipped. I had to come to terms with a lot of inner turmoil and self-doubt. My past experiences left me extremely vulnerable to criticism, and I desperately wanted to be approved by others. I was consumed with my performance and longed for those in leadership to validate me as a pastor and maybe even as a good man—something my father wasn't there to do for me. I lacked confidence, but at the same time, God was doing amazing things. People were inspired to go into the community and bring the church where it was needed the most.

I knew this outreach initiative had to look different from a typical church outreach. We were not going to do another outreach that was a picnic on our church grounds. We didn't want to get people in our church pews so we could convert them to givers. For me, outreach had to be us going into the most broken places where we expected no return on our investment. We had to go in and love people where they lived, just like Jesus did. The leadership of the church agreed and let me run with that vision. It was exciting but also a scary time. I felt unqualified most of the time, but God uses us the most when we are the least qualified or where He can get the credit He deserves for the results.

Working on staff at a church was intimidating. I found myself working with all the people on the stage I had looked up to as my pastors. I looked up to them all but when I got to know them, I learned they were just like everybody else. The lead pastor at that time took every opportunity to share my story from the stage, trying to leverage my experience for the good—to get people involved and to reach the lost.

As the outreach pastor, I ran into many people from my past. On one occasion, I was at an apartment complex in a poor area of town. I used to sell drugs close to that complex where we were now holding outreach block parties that included inflatables for the children and other fun activities. I was walking across the apartment complex when I heard some-one call my name. It was Mr. Bruner, an older African American gentleman, who had taken me under his wing in prison, giving me lots of good advice like not to gamble or not to borrow things from people, along with a lot of tips that kept me out of trouble.

When he got out of prison, he was still struggling with alcohol, but every time I came to the complex, we would sit down and talk. I walked with him through the death of his wife and other family members. When I went over to see him on this day, I gave him a big hug, but I could see his eyes were bloodshot even though it was only 10 AM. He said he looked across the complex and thought he had seen an angel when he saw me.

I informed Mr. Bruner I was not an angel, just a man who loved Jesus and him. He started weeping on my shoulder, saying, "My wife passed away. I can't stop drinking. I don't know what to do with myself. Would you come inside and pray with me and my family?"

I went inside and his place was full of gang members and weed smoke. They stood up and Mr. Bruner introduced me as his white son who was going to pray for everyone. We stood in a circle and I prayed my heart out for that family. I was grateful I could go back and speak into the communities where once I had done so many bad things. God was using me and giving me favor and influence in a broken community.

Once I was at Victory Church for a Wednesday night service, and many people were responding to an altar call. I looked up and saw a girl coming forward who had worked as a dancer and also sold drugs for me. She ran up to me, gave me a big hug, and started crying, explaining through tears, "I can't take this life anymore." She gave her life to Christ and I had the privilege of watching her transformed as she walked out her faith in Christ.

Because our church had a mission to reach the city with the good news of the Gospel, I saw many others I knew like that girl. Our pastor had a vision that our church was to be a hospital for those who didn't know Jesus and their place for healing. One time, he gave an altar call and a big, burly guy started barreling towards me with a brisk, aggressive-looking walk. I could hear him saying, "Hey Chappell. Hey Chappell." (When people call me Chappell, I know they are from prison, for everybody in prison calls you by your last name.) When he got closer, I immediately recognized him.

He thanked me for talking with him while we hung out at the weight pile whenever we were working out at Holdenville. I had befriended him and used to talk all that God stuff, as he called it. He said he heard the Word at the church and it lined up with what I had talked to him about in prison. He explained, "I just had to respond to this invitation and give my life to Christ."

I can't count how many people have found me through Facebook or have come to tell me that watching my life in prison transformed their lives. It's nothing I said or did. I didn't sit down with them and walk them through a prayer of salvation or anything like that. I simply befriended them because I wasn't intimidated by them. I thought they needed a Christian friend and not somebody who was trying to convert them. My philosophy has always been that if we would only build a relationship with people who aren't Christians, and maintain healthy boundaries as Christ followers with them, then we would see people transformed.

That's what Jesus did. He didn't just talk to people; He created intimate personal space with them. He crossed cultural and social boundaries and violated social taboos. It was overwhelming to see so many different people reach out to me and say they were impacted by my life, but I can't take any credit. I simply tell people that the Holy Spirit is good at doing

His job. We just show up and love people. It's foolish to think we can improve on the work of the Holy Spirit and what Jesus has already done. They are good on their own.

Then there's another man who I will call Thomas. I was in prison with him, and he was always saying things like, "Dude, thanks for being my friend. When I get out, I'm going to smoke weed and use meth casually so I can function." I would never judge what he said, and I remained his friend.

Recently we were painting the second location for City Center. My brother brought over a group of men from drug rehab to help us along with a volunteer who was not in drug rehab—he was just a volunteer who worked with my brother. It turns out that this young volunteer was Thomas' son. The son came up to me to say, "I want to thank you so much for the influence you had on my dad. I wouldn't have him in my life today if it wasn't for you befriending him in prison." I never in a million years thought that I would have a conversation like that with anyone. I am grateful for how God has used my story, my crazy life, and my dumb decisions for good to impact people.

What's more, Thomas regularly sends me messages on Facebook to say that the talks we had sitting on the prison run transformed his way of thinking. He recently wrote to report, "I'm a Christian now. I got out about a year ago and I own my own home. I've got a great job. I've been clean and sober for this amount of years."

An undeniable theme emerged again and again in my life. I repeatedly found myself back in similar places with similar people; only this time, I was completely different. I had been transformed. I had polluted our communities with drugs, but I was returning to those communities and touching lives for Christ. I was seeing people who participated in sin with me, but now we were serving our communities together. I had written love letters to God and given them to my mother, and now I was living out those love letters as an outreach pastor.

Those eight years in outreach ministry were full of special stories of God's faithfulness, but one day, it all came to an end as God revealed a new plan for our lives that was going to take us away from the city I loved, only to have us return a short time later.

CHAPTER NINE

Heading North

I was on staff at Victory for eight years and had established a rhythm of life and ministry. Our lives were consumed by all the activities common to a big, busy church, and I found much fulfillment in this place of influence where I was able to directly impact people's lives. I had responsibility for the church's outreach ministry, the security team, and the addiction and recovery ministry. I enjoyed being in the middle of so many opportunities to interact with people every week.

Unfortunately, the church experienced a

devastating blow upon discovering the misconduct and moral failure of our senior pastor, who was removed from his position. The pastor who took over, Jon Chasteen, is one of my closest friends and I was excited to serve under his leadership. At the same time, we were feeling like we needed to take a break and heal from all that had happened at the church. That's when a close friend of ours, CJ Johnson from Minnesota, reached out to us after he had taken the lead pastor role of a church that was meeting a high school at that time. He was proposing to add Julie and me as associate pastors to the team to help him and asked if we would be willing to come up to preach on a Sunday and consider the roles. We prayed about it intensely, flew up there, and I preached on a Sunday morning. I thought, *There's no way I'm going to move up here. I'm an Oklahoma City guy. This will a great time to reconnect with great friends and then get back to business in the city.*

That entire trip was amazing. We fell in love with the church and the staff and knew deep in our hearts serving this church was going to be our next season in life. God spoke to both Julie and me, and before we knew it, we were packed and moving to Minnesota to start a whole new chapter of our lives. When we knew we were supposed to move to Minnesota, we wept because we felt like we were going through a mourning process as we left the Church we loved so dearly. I laid on the couch for an entire day. I didn't want to miss the Lord and move out of His will, but I had an intense inner struggle over the entire transition.

I also felt like we were abandoning our church in a vulnerable time. The pain caused by the loss of the founding pastor was difficult for everyone. We came to realize that our move was necessary, however, more so for us to find a time of healing and to gain a new perspective on our lives. I felt like I was abandoning the staff I had served with for eight years and leaving some of my best friends to handle the transition without us. I was also one of the most tenured pastors there at the time. When I broke the news to Pastor Jon, it threw him for a major loop. Looking back, I think it was one of the most difficult conversations I ever had with such a close friend but, in hindsight, I knew it was exactly what I was supposed to do.

My former life intersected with my new life right up to the time we left the city. The week before we left for Minnesota, I was asked to speak at a gathering of first responders and law enforcement officials. It was right at the time when the tension began between law enforcement officers and different people groups in our nation. I shared my story with the crowd, thanking them for their service because they usually only see a lot of harsh and traumatic stuff.

I began by acknowledging that first responders were continually dealing with the worst scenarios our city offered and seldom got to see any positive things or hear about the good side of what they do. As first responders, they were regularly dealing with people who had either shot somebody or were shot by somebody. I wanted them to know that I was standing before them as an example of someone whose life can be changed and I was thankful for their efforts that saved my life. I stood before them as proof that there was good coming from their efforts to preserve life and serve the city.

Then I shared my story. After my speech, I met the first responders who saved my life. Our paths crossed 20 years ago in tragedy and now we were unexpectedly reunited for the common good of our city. What's more, the sergeant who booked me into the jail that day was present and he remembered the entire day. The whole story was written up on the front page of a newspaper in Oklahoma City and was released on a Saturday.

The next day was our last day at Victory Church before we were to leave for Minnesota. The church set aside a room for us so that people could come and say goodbye. There was a line out the door of possibly 1,000 people who came through and wanted to shake our hands, love on us, and thank us for being there. I was unaware of how many people cared about us and were aware of me and my story.

One of the people in line was a man with his wife who were both in tears. He told us, "I read your story in the paper and I knew I had to come and meet you. Today, after I heard the message and your story, I gave my life to Christ. I don't think I'm ever going to be the same again." What a going-away gift that some man would read the article, and respond by giving his life to the Lord. After that, we uprooted to a new place in Minnesota where I knew no one and no one knew me. We packed up our lives and went north, moving into the basement of our friend's and lead pastor's house to begin our new life. They were gracious enough to let us live in the basement to save some money while we were looking for a home of our own.

As I said, it was a necessary journey. We went from a very large church that had a great deal of influence in the community through the outreach ministry, and I was the pastor who led this ministry. I was the pastor who had been in prison with the crazy story of redemption. The founding pastor of the church in Oklahoma would share that story often to give people hope for their futures. An unhealthy identity in my position as a pastor developed in me and moving to Minnesota proved later to be one of the healthiest things that could have happened to me.

Even though my heart was in the right place, it was interesting to look back and see how a position in ministry had become my identity. Before I knew it, I had accumulated a burden and weight I didn't need. This was what I did, not who I was. I didn't realize how those things had embedded themselves in me. I think if every pastor was honest, they would admit to that dynamic. It was a beautiful thing to go up north and to have some of that stuff removed from my heart.

My wife and I were able to work closely in ministry together in Minnesota, which prepared us for what we're doing now at City Center. My wife and I grew together as we pastored people side-by-side and served the church. We were in Minnesota for about a year and a half and fell in love with many of the people in the church. We have dear friends to this day with whom we stay connected. It's crazy how connected we still are to that church. We go up there at least twice a year and enjoy every moment there with our friends.

As time went on, however, I began to feel a void. My heart ached for the opportunity to love and serve people living on the fringes of society in Oklahoma City. I became restless and started to drive for Uber in the Twin Cities. I had to find a demographic similar to the people I missed in Oklahoma. A restlessness was wearing on me and growing stronger each day. I wasn't sure what to do with the weight of it all.

Julie and I began to pray with great intensity once again about what to do. We loved the staff and people of this healthy, thriving church where we felt so at home. It was one of the most rewarding experiences we ever experienced with the staff and the lead pastors. We simply felt like there was a void in the ministry of which we were still to be a part. Then out of the blue, Pastor Jon from Oklahoma invited me back home to speak and during that visit, asked me, "What would you think if you had a building, a place to operate some type of center, a place where you could reach people in the community who are broken and hurting?"

I told him, "You're describing my dream job." We began to speak more in-depth about the prospects of doing something like this and I said, "Let's do it. Let's pull the trigger." Three weeks later, on August 1, 2016, we were moving back to Oklahoma City to take on yet another new endeavor. We hit the ground running and began preparing the legal papers for City Center with the generous blessing and support of our Minnesota church family and our Victory Church family.

Our Minnesota church supports our work in Oklahoma, often sending teams down to work with our youth. We had one of the most life-changing experiences on staff up north and cherish what God did in us during that season. Pastor CJ and Kristin are still among our closest friends and the church serves as a haven we can go to when we need to rest and relax. (Southland City Church is worth a visit if you find yourself near Rosemount, Minnesota). As great as Minnesota was, however, it was time to go home.

CHAPTER TEN

Coming Home

As I explained earlier, I became restless and realized I am drawn to people on the fringes of society who are difficult to reach. Julie and I are passionate about reaching families and vulnerable young people at risk, and Oklahoma City was ripe with those who fall into this category. When I looked at my Facebook and Instagram feeds, I saw numerous stories confirming that the youth in Oklahoma were among the most underserved youth in our nation. I also read how the education system in Oklahoma was failing them. Pockets of poverty in Oklahoma were being compared with situations in some developing countries, and I was stressed about it.

Justifiable anger rose within me, and I thought, *What is going on with our city? This is my city.* The more I thought about it, the more convinced I was that we had to figure out a way to have more of an impact in the community we loved so deeply. In our initial discussions, Pastor Jon offered me the church's old south building along with significant seed money to develop the kind of organization that could help serve our city.

Ever since I began walking with Jesus, I've realized I have a purpose in Christ. It's been something that's deep inside of me. It began to emerge years ago when I was driving downtown with a close friend and colleague while on staff at Victory Church. Coincidentally enough, it was CJ, the pastor from Minnesota who used to be on staff with me in Oklahoma! As we drove, we went past a huge cathedral and he said, "Someday you should acquire a building like that and make it an outreach center." His comment struck me as humorous. I was a brand-new pastor trying to figure out what it would even look like for me to be in ministry. I would ask myself if I was doing it all correctly. *Am I supposed to be doing this? Am I called to be a pastor?* I was deeply impacted that someone else would see something in me that I didn't see in myself at that time.

Over the years while I served as a pastor, my sense of purpose began to evolve inside of me. I thoroughly loved the outreach activities I did for the church. I knew the body of Christ in our city could alter our tragic statistics if we could have a separate entity for the church, but outside the church. I knew it had to be its entity so it could involve other churches and bring unity among all the other parts of the body of Christ throughout the city.

My wife and I would dream about something like a center similar to a family resource center that would initially affect and begin the connection process with the youth. With Jon on board to help launch this vision as we headed home to Oklahoma City, I explained to him that there was much we could accomplish in Oklahoma City to be an answer to a difficult problem, but it could not be connected to any one church. I had learned that the capital "C" church, in general, had abdicated its responsibility in our problem communities for too long. Perhaps not intentionally, but we had surrendered the initiative of social justice to other organizations and entities. I wanted to provide a vehicle where the church could come in and help serve the community.

He said, "It sounds like you have been thinking about this for a while." I laughed and told him I had—for about ten years. I knew our city could be beautiful, but the initiative could not be the program emanating from one single church, but rather needed to be a multi-church, multi corporation, multi-foundation, multi-individual sponsored initiative. It could not have a church's name attached to it for the simple reason that churches are competitive. I watched many multi-church efforts lose support if a single church was sponsoring or underwriting the outreach event.

As an outreach pastor, I would wrestle with frustration when we sponsored an event to reach the community. It was near impossible to get another church involved if they weren't the primary, funding sponsor. I knew our Center had to be a legitimate and separate organization. Any and every church would have to release the idea that this was going to be their thing. It was going to be God's thing. It was going to be an autonomous organization, and we had to raise our own money and pay our bills. Pastor Jon agreed. Without his willingness to support the Center and forfeit acknowledgment of his church, this project would not be where it is today. He's been generous and openhanded, and it's rare to see that kind of servant leadership these days.

Three weeks after that conversation with Jon, we were on the road back to Oklahoma City. It was a whirlwind of a time and honestly, one of the greatest challenges was leaving our relationships up north. We could have easily seen ourselves spending the rest of our lives there. It was such an amazing environment to live in. The friends we have up there still today are authentic, and we lived a picturesque, Norman-Rockwell-type life. Despite all that, we knew we were called to something great back home when it involved serving our marginalized friends in the city.

I don't want to sound like what we do here is more admirable than what they were doing up there. It's not; it's all Kingdom work. We all have our specific callings, but I know for us, our work at the Center is what we are supposed to do. It's not only what we're supposed to do, but it's also what we were born to do. I feel like we're in a place of favor. The culmination of all the circumstances in Julie's and my life and everything that we've ever done or hoped for is in what we are currently doing.

Our goal was to establish a safe, neutral, and common ground—a community center for families and youth to come where they could receive the resources they need. Ultimately, the hope was to have a one-stop-shop to meet any and every need that exists in under-resourced communities in Oklahoma City. It is difficult to get around in OKC because the transit system is awful and that's why we believe there should be a center like ours for each square mile of an under-resourced community so people can walk to it.

I wear many hats since the Center is in its infancy. I am trying to move out of anything and everything that's not related to fundraising, leadership, vision, and strategy. I have devoted much of my time so far in developing and instilling our leadership philosophy within our site leadership team while also casting vision, developing strategy, donor relations, and fundraising. God is using my story on a large scale to see this vision come to pass.

As we work, I feel like we have the lungs of a marathon runner and the legs of a sprinter. We're running a marathon at a dead sprint but not getting tired. I know exactly who I am, where I am supposed to be, and what I am to be doing. I embrace and am aware of my strengths and weaknesses. I'm not trying to label myself or ever put any limit on who I am based on my past experiences, but only on who I am in Christ. Through that filter, I am living the best life God has called me to live.

Many people see the value of what we're doing, and they realize what we are doing has produced results because we address the needs of the community. For example, we've put too much pressure on our educators. They shouldn't have to be worrying about kids being fed. They need to worry about educating young people. The breakdown and failure have come from broken families and broken systems. We can provide relief for this pain. We can help solve the lack of clothing or food and the lack of social or spiritual development our kids are experiencing. We can send these kids to school healthy, whole, and focused, so educators can then do what they're supposed to do. The city, the education system, and the nonprofit world see how viable our centers are and can be.

It's not just about City Center. It's about partnering with multiple organizations to see how we can collectively have an impact. By sharing measurements and space, having a level of trust with one another, and maintaining high levels of communication, we can effectively measure the impact we are having within the community together. With what we're trying to accomplish, our collective impact hopes to gather multiple organizations in multiple neighborhoods into the one bright beam that can shine in our communities and help heal them.

God's has poured out His favor on us in this organization. It's been exciting to see how God can use a knucklehead like me with the DOC number to stand in the middle of a boardroom and cast vision for the future. Then I can put on some Chuck Taylor's and jeans and speak to an angry young person. It's been exciting to watch the whole process unfold.

CHAPTER ELEVEN

The Center

When we first came back to Oklahoma City, we identified a board of directors and established bylaws so that we could file for our 501(c)(3) non-profit organization status through the IRS. Julie and I talked every day about what we could accomplish, encouraging one another and dreaming about how we were going to occupy the building. People who knew me from the outreach days at Victory Church were eager to hear what we were going to do and there was a big buildup of excitement and anticipation. We wanted people in our city to take ownership of the vision for the Center and take responsibility to love their city.

When we finally announced what we intended to do, the momentum exploded. Our announcements went viral on social media and many people signed up to volunteer and get involved. In the meantime, we were busy outlining and establishing different programs and initiatives. Victory Church let us use their old church building for a low rental cost. About 300 volunteers completely gutted, painted, and decorated it. We got the building prepared even though only about a third of those folks had specific construction skills, but they all had a heart to work.

As we walked through that process, we were engaging and inspiring more and more people to be part of this initiative we were calling City Center. We published our mission statement and got our website up. News outlets came and did stories on us. Even before the doors opened, we had people coming in who needed our services. We started helping single moms and young people before we had any programs or staff. The floors weren't even completed and we didn't have furniture, but we had an immediate response as a result of the obvious needs in the community. As word spread about what we were doing, still more people got involved, along with entire churches and organizations.

This is what we wanted to see happen. We wanted a safe, neutral ground for anyone and everyone who wanted to do good in the community or needed to receive some help. The culture at City Center creates space where everyone can function shoulder to shoulder and see eye to eye. We are not the benevolent, do-good church folks serving those poor disadvantaged people; we are all in it together. We are not better than those who need help. We realize that those of us who have resources and the ability to help have a lot to learn from the community we are called to serve. God is giving us opportunities to empower them with what we already have in our possession, but they have something to teach us too.

People who come to us for help often don't realize they have assets and skills that will help others. We didn't open the Center to show the community residents that we had something to make them better. We wanted to help them see that they had something in their hands that could build and serve their community. With the perspective of mutually adding value to one another, we are seeing an amazing process of restoration take place and growing exponentially. As I write, we're preparing to open a second location in a few weeks. We have eight total staff members between the two locations, and God keeps surprising us time and again.

I refer to City Center as an under-resourced family and at-risk youth center. It is designed to lock arms with other organizations like churches, corporations, nonprofits, and agencies in the community to work under one roof while maintaining their own identity. We hope to have a significant impact in any community where a Center is located. The ultimate goal is to open a Center every one or two miles apart within other under-resourced communities in Oklahoma City. Right now, we've identified 11 severe pain points with high crime rates in our city where we feel like these resource centers would be helpful. We are setting up central offices and developing a strategy of scale to implement new locations of hope in Oklahoma City.

Our staff arrives at about 9 AM when we get together to pray. We ask God to move and use us as we implement our programming and strategies to reach and mentor at-risk youth. Throughout the day during the school year, we see families come in needing food and clothing, or some type of support resource. We find ways to connect those families with what they need. We allow them to grab frozen family meals we have been prepared or to shop in our clothing closet. They can grab a food box and pick up hygiene items, and as needed, they can connect with our resource partners in the building. We have a connection with community social services who will come and operate from our building regularly. We have a resource register where families can learn about other social service agencies if that agency is not already at our facility on a specific day.

Our staff is flexible, fluid, and versatile in their ability to receive people because we never know what kind of needs will be presented. When the after-school program kicked off, there was a lot of controlled chaos. We reminded ourselves that if this was easy, everyone would be doing it. It's difficult when people come with big suitcases full of challenges and needs, but we receive them.

In the beginning, we decided that we were going to show them grace and love as we initiated a relationship with them, affirming them as human beings. We did this and as the relationships developed, we began to establish healthy boundaries helpful for our youth who normally don't have boundaries. We gradually add more boundaries and structure, and then go farther and have a structured time that begins to shape the after-school sessions.

We knew that in some ways we were being taken advantage of when we first started to build our relationships with those who come. We go into it knowing that we will give of ourselves and open our lives to these kids, and it may never be returned or appreciated. However, we choose to look at it from a different perspective. I knew from personal experience that our youth can spot a fake in a minute. We had to be real and demonstrate that we loved them and were there for them. After a while, we started to see the trust established. Now we have a leadership team dedicated to serving our youth along with a ton of volunteers who help us shape these young people's lives.

We have about 150 youth a day who come to our after-school program, and we are serving about 1,000 meals a week. Our mission states that we bring relief and restoration to lives, so it doesn't end with a meal, a sandwich, or a coat giveaway. Everything must lead to an ongoing path for restoration through relationships. All that we do—whether it's mentorship through our education room or our athletic program, whether through our clothing closet, our feeding program, or our nutrition program—is a conduit to build and strengthen relationships.

Too often our help comes in the form of rules. We want them to automatically respond to our rules without making any effort to build a relationship. This doesn't work. Through relationships, strong bonds are established, and only then do the youth make significant progress in their lives. We know we can guide them in a direction in which their lives can be turned around.

Not only do we work to establish relationships with the community, but also with our other ministry partners. Let me tell you about a few of those partners. One is a nonprofit partner organization named STORM, which stands for Strategic Treatment Options and Recovery Ministries and is led by our friends, George and Meredith Schaefer. George is a retired Army veteran who came home with a nasty case of PTSD, along with multiple other diagnoses. He found no help from his Army company and could not locate any other solutions, even though he needed immediate help. He fought through multiple addictions and after three years of being clean, he and his wife formed STORM to provide help for any family in crisis due to drug addiction. Specifically, they have a passion for helping Army vets.

If a family comes to STORM wanting to get clean they probably don't know that STORM serves as a first responder for an addiction crisis. STORM's presence in the center is important because we don't have the time or skill to handle something of this nature, so we make a place for them to make their services available, providing them space in the building so they can respond to those needs.

We also have agencies that offer social services to DHS clients, such as the Department of Human Services Child Welfare. These workers come in to meet and counsel with some of our youth, most of whom are within the scope of the agency's purpose and need their services. These counselors come and spend most of their day trying to find ways to get our young people clothes, food, and other necessities.

At least once a day during the week, I get a report that one of our kids (ages 8 to 14) is struggling with suicidal thoughts. The counselors are busy trying to find them the necessities of life like clothes and food when they should be counseling them on more important matters. Now we have clothes in the clothing closet and food in our kitchen so we can meet all their needs while they're here. Now they can sit down and talk with the counselors about their suicidal thoughts. Our partnership with them is making a difference.

We also work with Dragonfly Home, a nonprofit organization fighting human trafficking. They conduct training with our youth that focuses on Internet safety. There are so many creeps out there on social media who are looking to ensnare and then traffic youth. (One of the primary sources of sexual trafficking is social media.) Our kids are vulnerable and tend to respond more often to online invitations because they're hungry and think, *Why not go hang out with a guy who drives an expensive car? At least he will feed me at McDonald's.* We are educating at-risk youth and their families through that kind of partnership. They also bring ladies from a rescue home to our building to use the gym for yoga.

We partner with another group called the Sparrow Project, which does an excellent job of training our volunteers to understand the context and culture of those we serve. If we are going to serve people in an under-resourced community, we must train the well-meaning suburbanites coming to volunteer to understand three things.

First, they must be educated that their money is not the only answer. Second, they need to understand the culture. For example, respect looks a lot different to a middle-aged, white man living in suburbia than it does to a 16-year-old, African-American youth living in the urban community. The inner-city kid may be living with and raised by his or her 80-year-old grandmother, and maybe hasn't eaten in three days. In their culture, respect looks completely different than it does to the kid raised in the suburbs. We conduct extensive, volunteer training partnering with the Sparrow Project.

We work with another group called Edmond Mobile Meals. They come in and teach kids to create nutritious meals out of basic shelf staples they can get anywhere or that we can give them. When they are trained, they know how to cook safely even if they're home alone. Those are just a few examples of the many partnerships we already enjoy at City Center.

There was a time when my role at the Center involved anything from designing a graphic to sitting in a board meeting asking for money. When we first started, Julie and I were involved in every detail and function of the organization. I realized that this was not sustainable, but it was necessary to get things started. Now my primary role is leadership over the staff as CEO, but I still struggle to maintain a healthy balance.

I believe that my past has allowed me a unique perspective and a strong voice into the conversation surrounding community transformation. I realize my weaknesses. I need help in converting the vision into a functional group of systems that propel the organization forward. I feel we have put the team together to do just that.

If someone punches a person in the arm, a bruise develops because all the blood flows to the pain point in the body to help it heal. That's exactly how we see ourselves helping the city to heal—that's why we call our current and future locations pain points. Typically, churches over time have made the choice to retreat to areas of prosperity so they can thrive. There must be another organization to fill the void where those churches used to be. Churches can't always be in the pain points of our city because there are no finances to sustain them. There must be an organization like ours through which the church can see help, hope, and healing flow to these pain points. I feel like that's what we do.

We are the pain seekers so we can be the avenue through which the church works to bring healing and hope. I tell people all the time that there's nobody else coming. As Christ-followers, until He returns, we are the cavalry coming to the rescue. Nobody else is coming with the healing truth of the Gospel who can respond to the needs and relieve the pain and hurt in our community with viable solutions. If not us, then who? The answer is nobody.

Jesus said that we would all do greater things in His name. Now that He's gone, He sent the comforter, the Holy Spirit, to us. I'm always trying to figure out, *How are we going to do greater things than Jesus?* The answer is that we will do the greater things by being agents of change within the pain points of our communities. I'm bound and determined to see, provoke, and inspire other people in the power of the Holy Spirit so it can happen.

In addition to my work at the Center, I feel called to challenge, equip, and mobilize the Church for action. The Church needs to be provoked and maybe even poked in the eye. We could do what we are attempting to do for our distressed communities with greater excellence if the body of Christ as a whole would come together and marshal their resources.

CHAPTER TWELVE

Three Lessons

The message of this book that resonates with my wife and me is that we serve a full-circle God who wants to use everything we experience and pick up along the way for something specific. I regularly return to reflect and speak on Jeremiah 29:11: "'For I know the plans I have for you,' declares the Lord, 'plans to prosper you and not to harm you, plans to give you hope and a future.'" That's a verse we all love to hear because it gives us hope in what otherwise may be a hopeless situation.

If you read the previous verses leading up to

that verse, however, you realize that it's not a promise with immediate results. There was a process the children of Israel had to walk through to see that promise fulfilled. I lived through that process and watched as God fulfilled His promise to me, bringing both my past and my present into one seamless, redemptive story. Therefore, I encourage people with the truth that everything they are going through now is building them up for something great God has for them. The justice of God's love and forgiveness motivates me to make things right in the communities we touch through our Centers.

The concept of forgiveness is an important part of my life and message. There are other things I emphasize, but forgiveness is vital if anyone is to walk in the fullness of life Christ has for them. If we don't truly embrace forgiveness and walk it out every day, checking our hearts for its presence, then we can get into big trouble.

If we go back to the beginning of Jeremiah's message, we see that he was refuting another prophet who was speaking false things—predicting God was going to relent from His message of judgment and thus everything was going to be alright. Jeremiah responded that the people were going to stay in exile, so they should settle down and make the best of it— marry, plant crops, and pray for the people of Babylon who were oppressing them. They were going to be there for seventy years, so their exile would not be over any time soon. There was no quick or easy fix and the people needed to make the most of their opportunities to live, love, and grow.

This reality was discouraging to the Israelites

because they had been raided, mocked, and abused, being carried away to a foreign land. They never dreamed this would ever happen to them—God's chosen people, but it did, and they found themselves living in a land far away from their beloved homeland. I've learned that God's plan for our lives is certain and inevitable, but not always immediate—and not without some pain of preparation and unmet expectations along the way.

In my situation, I wanted God's plan to unfold immediately during my first two years in prison. I thought, *Okay God, my sin has been forgiven and I have been made right by your saving grace. You're in my heart and life. I know You're good, but help me to see your plan here. I'm 19 years old; I still have a long life ahead of me. Help me get out of here.*

As my relationship matured with the Lord, I realized I had to partner with God's plan (not control it) and that together we would engage in activities benefitting other people. God's plan gradually began to unfold, but in the meantime, I had to cling to the promise in Jeremiah 29:11: "For I know the plans I have for you, plans to prosper you and not to harm you, plans to give you hope and a future." God promised me a future, but I had to embrace and cooperate with His plan to get me there.

God's plan for all of us requires patience. Israel had to mature and learn from their mistakes, which required them to settle down in Babylon and get focused on learning lessons there. God wanted to establish something in their hearts and lives, and that included endurance and perseverance. I had to release the temptation to figure a way out of prison as soon as possible. I had to be patient and settle in.

As I engaged in appropriate and needed programming and training, and established relationships with the right people around me, I learned to understand myself and why I made some of the choices I did. I identified the root causes that fueled the terrible decisions I had made as a teenager. As I became patient, God worked His forgiveness in my life. I grew to appreciate the process God was leading me through.

After I resolved to be patient and trust God to let Him do His work in my heart, I realized my life was about a much bigger story—a collective story. God showed me the importance of sharing my experience of what He had done in my life because it had tremendous value for other people. I did not learn this in the classroom; I learned it through the awkwardness and, at times, the messiness of community. My relationships continued to demonstrate and remind me of God's grace in my life.

I had the opportunity to take college courses in prison and received most of my college education while I was there. There was an inmate in some of my classes named Butch (not his real name). Butch was serving a life sentence for murder and was about ten years older than I. He was a law clerk and a slick-talking guy. When I met Butch, he had been in prison for 25 years, entering prison when he was about 16 years old (he was tried and convicted as an adult due to the nature of his crime). Butch was a guy who worked the system, always trying to get out on a technicality.

Butch and I developed a good relationship (my strategy to influence others for Christ). I didn't try to get Butch to agree with me or align with my beliefs or anything like that. He knew I was a Christ-follower. He would acknowledge and respect that in the conversations we had, but would ask me, "Why do you believe like that? I don't even know if God is real." At other times, he would proclaim, "God's not trying to do anything for you. He's probably not even real." None of that intimidated or concerned me. We continued to talk often and had a cordial relationship.

When I got out of prison, I concluded, *Butch is never getting out of prison. He stabbed people while he was in and committed other crimes while he was incarcerated. There is no way they are ever going to let him out even though he thinks he can find a loophole.*

I had been a pastor for a short time and was at a 7-Eleven store when I heard somebody call my name, "Hey Chappell," indicating we had known one another in prison. I couldn't discern from the tone whether this person was happy to see me or not, and thought, *Oh man, this could be anything,* but when I looked over my shoulder, it was Butch.

I said, "Butch, did you break out of prison? How are you able to be standing here right now?"

He had a big smile on his face and said, "Chappell, I continually think back on all those conversations we had. I know they weren't deep or real theological, but I need you to know I chose to follow Jesus. I've been out now for two years and I'm married. It was a miracle I got out, and I wandered into a church one day and found everything we had talked about. It all just sort of clicked and made sense to me. I just want to say thanks for being my friend and talking to me when I was a pretty difficult person to talk to." He was correct. In prison, it was one f-bomb after another coming from his mouth. It was a normal language for him back then.

God was using all the extra time I spent in prison so He could use me to touch a few people in the prison yards, in the units I slept in, and in the college classes I attended. It wasn't about me getting out, it was about me staying in so God could develop me while at the same time use me to reach others. My life was not my own; it was and is His.

God is looking for people to serve as conduits and expressions of His love. I referred earlier to the words of Jesus: "Very truly I tell you, whoever believes in me will do the works I have been doing, and they will do even greater things than these because I am going to the Father" (John 14:12). That verse always challenges me. As I interpret it, He sent the Holy Spirit to dwell within us while we operate as vessels to express the love of Christ.

Even after I got out, God reminded me He would use my experiences to help others, and I was not to be hesitant to share them. After my time on staff at Victory Church, I converted a house I owned into what I called a sober-living house. My goal was to help some of the guys coming to the church who needed a place to live with a healthy environment so they could learn, stay sober, and get jobs. This proved to be a lot harder than I initially anticipated.

I would make it a point to take new residents on outreach to serve our city together and to spend some quality time getting to know one another. I thought of it as a day mission when we would spend half a day helping the elderly install a new garage door opener, or picking up trash, or mowing someone's lawn. It was always a good time for me to connect with the guys and tell them my story, encouraging them through what I had experienced. One resident was about five years younger than I. I felt he had a great chance to stay sober, and he was making plans to lead a successful life.

As I drove this promising young man around town, I told him my story. I have a video on my phone of the local news story on the day I was shot. It shows me on a stretcher violently convulsing after they had just saved my life and were taking me to the hospital. I told the young man, "This is me. This is where the bitterness in my heart took me. This is where unforgiveness led me. I know what it's like and I know how you feel. You're not talking to a guy who can't relate."

On the video, they had just shocked me with the defibrillator to revive me and it showed one of the paramedics putting a bag over my mouth and nose to keep me breathing. The young looked at the image of the guy bagging me and shouted, "Stop! Dude, that's my dad! My dad's been a paramedic for a lot of years." We watched the footage again to confirm what he had seen. Sure enough, it was his dad.

I asked if he realized the craziness of this moment. "Do you realize your dad saved my life and now we're sitting here, connected to this opportunity for you to live your life in sobriety. Look at how God uses our lives to benefit others. Even though you've been guilty of many past mistakes and poor decisions, all this stuff has happened to work His forgiveness into your life and to benefit others—if you let it." He said, "You're right. I can see that." From that moment on, he got the picture.

A final observation I take from Jeremiah 29:11 is that once we have patience and grasp the idea that this life is not only about us, but about God's restoration in others, then God can bring things full circle and then we fully come to understand that God is a full-circle God. Our lives are not linear, but circular. I can look at my future and think it's a straight line for me to get from here to there. God says, "No. We're still going to get there, but it's not going to be the straight shot you think it is. There are things you need to go around and more things you need to experience before you see my promise breakthrough in your life."

I look at my life and there are so many full-circle moments: with the officer who shot me, with the paramedic's son, the fact we own where I had my first volunteer experience as a wide-eyed ex-convict, and the open door for me to speak at Roosevelt, my former middle school from which I was expelled. My life has been a graphic illustration of how God brings things full circle.

God wants the best for us—more than we want the best for ourselves. Sometimes we feel we must strive and push and make things happen because we need to help God accomplish what's best for our lives. When we do, we end up falling flat on our faces. When we allow God's path to unfold, we understand His best is much greater than the best we can do for ourselves. That's something I learned from my personal experience with everything I have gone through. This is the lesson I had to learn, a lesson my process gave to me.

I have had to confront many issues in my life as I walked through a process of healing, but of all the issues, unforgiveness was the most difficult and the most important to learn. Allow me to share that learning experience with you in the next chapter.

CHAPTER THIRTEEN

Unforgiveness

I eventually came to understand that unforgiveness was the root of many issues and problems in my life. I had deep bitterness and unforgiveness toward one of my brothers and had a difficult time forgiving him for what I saw him do to my mom and me. Forgiving my brother didn't seem fair. I didn't ask for that trouble. I was innocent, only a kid and vulnerable. I felt validated in my feelings of anger and unforgiveness towards him. It wasn't fair that he did what he did, but it was fair that I felt the way I did.

One day, I realized that unforgiveness only

hurts the one who harbors it. It's like squeezing broken glass and expecting not to get cut. It's like drinking battery acid and hoping the other person feels it. Unforgiveness destroys us from the inside out. I learned forgiveness is a process I had to embrace every day. It was not a one-and-done thing.

Early in my faith walk, I had the impression I was going to come to the altar, ask for healing for something, and it would be gone. If it wasn't gone with no residue, then I thought something was wrong with me—perhaps I didn't have enough faith. That's not the case. Both our sanctification (being made holy) and healing are a process with specific steps we must accept. The healing journey was one I had to be willing to take. I had to pray for those people who had hurt me, even when they didn't deserve or ask for it. Then I had to forgive myself. This was difficult too, perhaps the least obvious step but at times the toughest one.

I'll be honest with you: When it came to praying for my brother, at first I didn't even mean the prayers I said. I prayed for him in church, saying things like, *God, I'm just going to say something in my head but it's not in my heart. I know the right things to say, but I don't mean them. Help me get to the place where I mean it.* The more I prayed for my brother, the more it changed me, not him. Our prayers for others may not change them, but they will always change us. Until I could get beyond my bitterness, I could never embrace or enjoy a better future. My bitter past was keeping me down and holding me back.

God gave me techniques and clues to help me recognize my unforgiveness, and they are still effective today. When I see a person in public who has hurt me and I have a gut-wrenching feeling in my stomach, this is a sign of unforgiveness. When I see a person who looks like another person who has hurt me and I avoid that person, I know there is a good chance I have unforgiveness. I must address it whenever I have those encounters or when thoughts of those people come to mind. After I started doing that, I lived a lighter, freer, and fuller life. Praying for those people was a big step for me. I knew forgiveness wasn't fair, and it was a process—a vital process.

Forgiveness brings healing both in and around your life. When I reached out to the officer who shot me and asked him for forgiveness for putting him in that position, he, in turn, felt like he needed my forgiveness, and this full-circle moment happened when we realized we were connected. God's redemption was working in my life and directly impacting lives around me, and forgiveness was the key.

I was a pastor on staff at a large church when some of these things were being healed in my life. As a pastor, I was expected to be teaching these principles to others, but I was learning them myself. Most people, especially leaders, are often fearful of being vulnerable and honest about things like that. We must learn to identify with the people we are serving by being transparent and authentic.

People want to follow an authentic leader more than they want to follow a perfect leader. I've been embracing the process of authenticity, and it has been both powerful and painful. And in the process of embracing it, I have found healing—even transformation. Forgiveness was a big part of my walk with Jesus.

Jerry, the officer who shot me, received a whole lot of healing through forgiveness, and his family received a lot of healing too.

Ultimately, if forgiveness was fair, then we would all fail to qualify. God forgave us and sent His Son to die a horrible death on our behalf so we could be forgiven and have the shame of our sin lifted from us. Then we can face and find healing and restoration from the carnage of our mistakes. It's not fair we are forgiven for all we have done. Since that's true, how in the world can we harbor any unforgiveness towards someone else?

Forgiveness is an emotional topic with which we must come to grips. We know Jesus has pardoned us from our sins, but that can be a difficult act to follow when we must do the same for others who have done grievous things to us. For me, forgiveness and pardon have played out in my life spiritually, but also played out in my life tangibly with natural consequences. I learned a lot about forgiveness as I walked out of the process of obtaining a legal pardon from the State of Oklahoma.

In 2012, a paralegal clerk filed paperwork for me to petition the Pardon and Parole Board to receive a pardon. At first, I thought it didn't matter whether I was pardoned or not. I was doing my job as a pastor, and a pardon was not going to help me do that. She filed the paperwork, but they contacted me to say it wasn't complete, explaining what else they needed from me.

Let's fast forward to the end of my time at Victory Church. We made the difficult decision to move to Minnesota, and after that, we felt like we were mourning the loss of a loved one. Two days after we made the decision, we received a letter informing us that I had a hearing for a pardon on a specific date between 3 and 5 PM. We discovered that the process of petitioning for a pardon, although set in motion a few years earlier, was still being considered.

We had read that the percentage of pardon denials after 11 AM increases by 70% because, obviously, the committee is tired and hungry by then. They are also overwhelmed and jaded from all the stories they endured listening to throughout the day. My time slot was 3 to 5 PM. I ended up going before the Board dead last. Afterward, they told me I was the worst and most improbable case they had considered all year. It's comical considering that I didn't know what I was there for. After all, we had not even finished the paperwork.

During the two hours I sat in the courtroom, I listened to many stories, but everyone was denied a pardon. Some were denied after having been charged with writing bad checks ten years ago. I was thinking, *Why am I here? This is not going to happen and is a waste of my time.*

Once I got before the Board, I had two minutes to talk. There was a lady in the middle with two ladies to her right and two men to her left, but the one in the middle was leading the conversation. I had watched her grill people the entire time I was there. I didn't have a strategy, but I thought, *I'm just going to let it rip and tell my whole story. I have nothing to lose.* They all took a deep breath, leaned back in their chairs, crossed their arms, and said, "Well, Mr. Chappell. What have you got for us?" sounding like they were doing this as a formality.

They let me talk for 20 minutes. I never felt the Holy Spirit's presence as strongly as I did in that room, except for the time in the county jail cell when I surrendered to Jesus. When I was halfway through, three of the Pardon Board members began to cry. I told my whole story and the moment was surreal as the tone of the room shifted and emotions rose. They were all leaning forward in their chairs and listening intently.

As I wrapped up, the presiding lady unfolded her arms and took a more open posture. She thought for a moment and then said, "Mr. Chappell, I'll be honest with you. We all met this morning and reviewed your jacket. We saw that you have done great things in the community and how you have reconciled with the officers. I used to be a police officer who worked on the force with Officer Jerry. I know and talked to him. He had nothing but great things to say about you. I also know his wife and we have a great letter from her about you. She was part of the community review committee and her words carry a lot of weight."

"We decided this morning that our vote was going to be no because there's too much publicity associated with your case. Your case was a violent crime towards a police officer. It did not make any sense whatsoever to pardon you, and that was our decision. Now after hearing your story and seeing you face-to-face, my vote is yes. What do you all think?" She turned to them and they all agreed, making the vote unanimous. I was in tears and they were, too. I thought, *Maybe I should go up and hug them.* Then I thought better than to do it. I got up, thanked them, and walked out of the room.

Four weeks later, I was in Minnesota and the

human resources director from Victory Church called to say that the governor's assistant was trying to get in touch with me. She gave them my cell number and the governor's assistant called to let me know they were preparing the paperwork to approve my pardon, which usually took 90 days—but mine took only 26. After that, I received a complete pardon for all my crimes from the state of Oklahoma. That is an absolute miracle. The violent nature of my crime against a police officer almost ensures that I would never receive a pardon.

What a perfect picture that was of what Christ has done for us! He allowed the pardon for my crimes as an added illustration of His goodness and a vivid example of what He's done spiritually for all of us. He has pardoned us. He absolved all the guilt of our offense. How can we not forgive those who have harmed us? God knows it is going to be difficult for us to forgive some people, but He's modeled a clear process for us to follow through prayer, guidance from His Word, and the help of His Holy Spirit. My pardon serves as a tangible reminder that forgiveness must always be a vital part of my life in Christ.

Honestly, self-condemning thoughts still emerge when I think of some of the dumb decisions I made that affected my son and family. I remind myself that this too is covered by the blood of Jesus and is all forgiven. Those negative thoughts aren't helpful; I wasn't created to live with the shame. There are people in our lives who are still broken and hurting, and they may even bring up our past or hold it against us. All we can do is confess our wrongdoing, apologize for the ways we may have caused them pain, and walk-in forgiveness. Maybe then, they can be free as well.

CHAPTER FOURTEEN

Full-Circle God

There is no end to the stories I can share to prove that God is a full-circle God. In 2017, I was asked to speak at a drug rehab venue called Rob's Ranch. The man who invited me to speak formerly worked for the Fellowship of Christian Athletes (FCA) and had also served as the chaplain for the University of Oklahoma football team. This chaplain developed an opiate addiction and overcame it, but before he did, he got caught while serving as the team chaplain. When he worked for FCA and was raising funds for his salary, he would be invited into donor's homes to make presentations. While there, he would go through their medicine cabinets and steal opioids. He got caught in the home of a lawyer who called the police. The chaplain was arrested and the story made national headlines.

This is where the story gets interesting, for the lawyer befriended the chaplain and they formed a close relationship. The lawyer helped get the charges reduced even though he was the one who turned the chaplain in. What's more, he walked with the chaplain through the entire rehab process. They together went on to found a nonprofit organization to help others with addictions, and I am happy to report that the chaplain is healed and transformed. At this point, you may be wondering what this story has to do with me and the concept of God bringing people full circle. Let me explain.

As we were riding out to Rod's Ranch, the chaplain told me his story and said I would meet his friend the attorney at the evening meeting. When I got to the Ranch, I was introduced to many recovering addicts and a few other people who I could tell were not recovering addicts. I didn't know who the attorney was and my host didn't point him out. I assumed one of them was the lawyer. I told my whole story that night and noticed one older gentleman who was absorbed in what I was saying. As I spoke, his eyes got bigger and bigger and he was more animated as I went on. I thought, *Wow, I know my story has had an impact on people before, but what's up with this guy? This is unusual and getting a little weird.*

Of course, I talk about forgiveness and explain that it isn't fair whenever I am allowed to share my story. However, that particular night, the crowd was responsive, so I went on to tell about Officer Jerry and me being reconciled and how it was featured in a newspaper article. Again, the man I assumed was the lawyer was nodding his head in agreement with a look of wonder on his face. When I finished, he approached me.

"I had no idea you were the speaker tonight," he began. "When I met the chaplain and he stole from my home, I called the police on him. I knew he was going to have to do some prison time, and it's then that I picked up the newspaper and saw the article about you. I read how you and the police officer reconciled and at that moment, God convicted my heart and showed me that I needed to reconcile with Kent and help him get through his addiction. When I read your story, I knew I had to reach out to Kent, forgive him, and help him. Now we are together leading a nonprofit organization as a team and here I am meeting you."

Only God could help someone like the lawyer come to the radical conclusion that he was to help and not prosecute or persecute the thief who stole from his home. And only God could use my story to impact two men I had never met who would apply the lesson of forgiveness to their situation. God had brought me full circle from being a man who broke the law to a man who was forgiven and pardoned so I could help others experience the forgiveness of Christ. My forgiveness of Officer Jerry opened up the door for forgiveness in someone else's life.

I look at my life and often reflect on my traumatic experiences and dumb decisions. When they happened, my only goal was to get through them and survive. As I walked through their consequences, however, God took me in a different direction. I wondered why it wasn't just a straight shot to the solution or healing I sought. *Why is God taking me in a circle around all these various obstacles?* They were all character-building opportunities and God was preparing to use the things I was learning to help other people.

When I first went to prison, I was hoping to get away from my past life. I thought it was over and I was going to pursue point B, which was a straight road from where I was standing. Then I discovered that my point B was right next to my point A, and God had to take me in a large circle to get me to point B. It wasn't miles away from my point A; it was right next to it. When I circled back around and faced my pain and the process to be free, I found myself building my present life on top of my past life, as sordid as it was. My obedience to go through God's process allowed the chaplain, his lawyer friend, and countless other people to benefit from my story—the good, the bad, and the ugly of it.

I was carrying a gun and ultimately engaged in an extreme act of violence against a police officer that almost cost me my life. I experienced prison and drug addiction and now I'm back in Oklahoma City where it all began. I see people who are where I was, and I can help guide them back to a place of healing where they have purpose, value, and worth. I can help them see they can add value to the community and not take value from it.

You have probably had your full-circle moments

and experiences of which you are ashamed. Don't be ashamed any longer, for those broken places can initiate healing for many other people. Surrender them to Christ because He will use them all. I've seen it in my life. I've learned more from my bad decisions than from my good ones—as long as I submitted those decisions to Jesus. The Bible is clear that God is working all things work together for good for those who are called according to his purpose (see Romans 8:28). The full-circle moments are designed and used by Him. I see my life in this light, and I see others' lives in the same fashion.

As I write this conclusion early in the morning, a young man named Jeremiah is tapping on my window. He knows he's not supposed to be here until noon, but Jeremiah has learned to love the Center and we love him. If City Center didn't exist, Jeremiah could already be dead. I met him a year ago and he was carrying dope around in his backpack along with some guns. When Jeremiah first came, he was disrespectful. We knew he lived in a bad situation. His parents were not in his life, and he was being raised by his grandmother in her eighties. We learned he had experienced a lot of violence in his home life, and he's also caused some major problems in school. It's not hard to understand why he was acting out when he came to us.

We began to love him while establishing healthy boundaries. Once, those boundaries included asking him to leave the Center As he left, he called me a cracker (a derogatory term for a white person). It was comical to see his anger play out that way because it didn't affect me. I heard the term all the time in prison.

Today, Jeremiah still comes to and is welcome at the Center. He comes back for the love and affirmation we give him. His whole demeanor has shifted—although he still faces many challenges. One day, the local TV station came out to shoot a story about one of our groups called the Hot Topic Group. This group was extremely diverse—black kids, white kids, Asian kids—and one of the things we talk about in the group is diversity and racism, and how they manifest in our community.

When the news cameras came, our group topic of the day was racism. Jeremiah was there that day and he was going to participate in the video. My wife and I looked at each other and we were both thinking, *Oh no, what's he going to say or do?* We cringed but talked it over, concluding that he had come a long way and it was worth the risk for him to participate. Jeremiah sat next to me during the discussion with questions like, "What is racism? Have you ever been a victim of racism? Have you ever been racist? What is the solution?"

What followed was an incredible discussion with this diverse group of kids. It was eye-opening to hear how middle-school youth had experienced and were fully aware of racism toward themselves and where it existed in the community. When the question came up if anyone had ever acted racist towards someone, Jeremiah, who is a young black man, raised his hand and said, "Yes. Mr. Jed had to kick me out one day and as I was leaving I turned around and called him a racist name. This is something I had learned to do, but it's wrong. I want to be an answer and a solution to that problem right here at the Center."

I almost fell off my chair. How powerful it was that Jeremiah, on his own and through the love and affirmation he had received at the Center, came to some conclusions on his own about how he should behave, and what his life can and should look like if he chooses to make positive and right decisions. This is why we founded the Center and how God is using it. If safe spaces like City Center don't exist, then we can't have those conversations with kids early in life. We can't create opportunities with level playing fields for young men like Jeremiah.

Who knows, Jeremiah may become a director one day of his own Center. He'll look back and say, "Man, I should have been kicked out of this place. I called the founder a cracker." Instead, he'll be able to look another kid in the eye and say, "I know you're angry. I know you're hurt. I know it sucks that you are being raised by your grandmother who doesn't know what's going on in your life. I know you hate watching your little brother beating your sister up and selling dope and gangbanging. I lived the same life. Let me tell you what I learned in this process and how I've come full circle. In the same way, He used my pain, I believe God will be able to use all you are going through to bring healing into your life and the life of many others."

This life isn't about our individual stories; God is so much bigger than that. It's about others. I have told you my story, but it's God's story—a story He is telling through me. It's about how I learned to take the focus off me and put it on God and others. God hasn't used me despite my past; He used me because of it. He wants to encourage other people through what I have experienced and He will do the same with and for you. He is truly a full-circle God.

My hope in writing this book is that you will look at your life, or at the life of someone you love, and identify some pain points that shaped those lives. Then I hope you will consider relinquishing those pain points to Jesus. I encourage you to engage in the process of forgiving those who may have hurt you. The process of healing begins with prayer and submission to Jesus Christ. (I hope you will pray to receive salvation in Him if you haven't already.) Look at those pain points as opportunities to come full circle, not to come back to the pain but to understand how the pain molded and shaped you, and how God wants to use your pain to relieve someone else's pain. God doesn't want you to forget the pain of your past, but to address the pain and surrender it to Him. Then engage in the process of forgiveness, so you can circle back to those pain points and bring healing to similar areas of pain in other's lives.

We are all agents of hope once we have submitted to Christ. I don't care if you have the most boring on undramatic testimony, your life matters and is relevant—and will speak to someone else. When you follow this pattern of a process in your life, you can become an agent of hope to people through the experiences you have had.

Now that you have read my story, I also hope you realize that if God can save and use a guy like me, He can use anyone—even you. There is not much to me outside of Christ. I simply submitted my story to Him, and it has become His story. Anything good that comes from this story, or that benefits you, makes my story your story. If He can use me, He can use you or someone you love. He can use anyone who comes to mind who is going through a challenging time. More than that, their challenges add value, purpose, and significance to their lives. They can have an impact for good based on the negative experiences they have had. I love it whenever people say, "Okay! I thought I was done, but after hearing (and now reading) your story, I see nobody is ever done."

I always say if you're not dead, God's not done. If you have breath in your lungs, then God can still be active in your life and use you to help others. We are just one act of repentance away from activating God's ability to bring us full circle through our pain to a place of purpose and meaning.

Amen.

CONTACT JED CHAPPELL

www.jedchappell.com

jed.chappell@okcity.center

INSTAGRAM
@jedchappell

www.facebook.com/JedChappell

CITY CENTER
www.okcity.center